UNDERSTANDING
E. L. DOCTOROW

Understanding Contemporary American Literature

Matthew J. Bruccoli, *Editor*

UNDERSTANDING

E. L.
DOCTOROW

DOUGLAS FOWLER

UNIVERSITY OF SOUTH CAROLINA PRESS

For Suzanne

Copyright © 1992 University of South Carolina

130584

Published in Columbia, South Carolina, by the University of South Carolina Press

Manufactured in the United States of America

Library of Congress Cataloging-in-Publication Data

Fowler, Douglas.
   Understanding E. L. Doctorow / Douglas Fowler.
      p.   cm.—(Understanding contemporary American
      literature)
   Includes bibliographical references and index.
   ISBN 0-87249-819-0 (alk. paper)
   1. Doctorow, E. L., 1931–   —Criticism and interpretation.
I. Title.   II. Series.
PS3554.O3Z65   1992
813'.54—dc20   92–8042

CONTENTS

Understanding Contemporary American Literature has been planned as a series of guides or companions for students as well as good nonacademic readers. The editor and publisher perceive a need for these volumes because much of the influential contemporary literature makes special demands. Uninitiated readers encounter difficulty in approaching works that depart from the traditional forms and techniques of prose and poetry. Literature relies on conventions, but the conventions keep evolving; new writers form their own conventions— which in time may become familiar. Put simply, *UCAL* provides instruction in how to read certain contemporary writers—identifying and explicating their material, themes, use of language, point of view, structures, symbolism, and responses to experience.

The word *understanding* in the series title was deliberately chosen. Many willing readers lack an adequate understanding of how contemporary literature works; that is, what the author is attempting to express and the means by which it is conveyed. Although the criticism and analysis in the series have been aimed at a level of general accessibility, these introductory volumes are meant to be applied in conjunction with the works they cover. Thus they do not provide a substitute for

Editor's Preface

the works and authors they introduce, but rather prepare the reader for more profitable literary experiences.

M. J. B.

UNDERSTANDING
E. L. DOCTOROW

"What happens is that you do something and only then do you figure out what it is," E. L. Doctorow once commented. "You write to find out what you're writing."[1] The author of *Ragtime, The Book of Daniel*, and *Billy Bathgate* is difficult to classify. In Doctorow's work there is no facile imitation of familiar types and no recycling of standard themes. No two of his novels seem at first glance to be alike. The reader's challenge and reward lie in trying to crystallize the set of laws and constants that govern Doctorow's fiction from beneath the surface.

Doctorow has been described as a "radical Jewish humanist" in sensibility, and he is proud of the label, even telling one interviewer that "if I was not in that tradition, I would certainly want to apply for membership."[2] He was born in New York City during the Depression, 6 January 1931, and into a heritage with a strong radical bias. He characterizes the milieu as "a lower-middle-class environment of generally enlightened, socialist sensibility."[3] Doctorow describes his paternal grandfather as "a printer, an intellectual, a chess player, an atheist, and a socialist."[4] The important writers on the home bookshelf were the prophetic-radical Jack London of *War of the Classes* and *The Iron Heel*; the "Great Agnostic" Robert Ingersoll with his rationalist critique of the Bible; and Herbert

Spenser, who argued for a progressive evolution-
ary tendency in human history. "I remember my
grandfather giving me Tom Paine's critique of fun-
damentalism, *The Age of Reason*, when I was ten or
eleven. And this continued with my father."[5]

Doctorow's charming but financially un-
steady father is one of the most appealing portraits
in his son's autobiographical novel, *World's Fair*.
The senior Doctorow had owned a radio, record,
and musical instrument store in Manhattan (the
family resided in the Bronx); after losing his business in the Depression, he kept his family afloat by
becoming a salesman of home appliances, and
later of television sets and stereo equipment.

After graduating from the Bronx High School
of Science in 1948, Doctorow went on to Keynon
College in Ohio. "There were lots of poets on campus, poetry was what we did at Kenyon, the way
at Ohio State they played football,"[6] Doctorow has
one of his characters say. He had in fact chosen to
go to Kenyon in order to study with the poet and
essayist John Crowe Ransom. As one of Doctorow's alter egos puts it, "To this day I don't understand how I had known about Ransom, how I as a
teenager could have made this knowledgeable
choice and found my way to central Ohio. Perhaps
my high-school guidance counselor saw in my
New York folk-singing background the makings of
a good Southern Agrarian."[7]

Still, Doctorow ended up majoring in philos-
ophy, not English, and acting in campus dramatic

productions instead of pursuing a literary apprenticeship and an academic career. After graduating
in 1952 he studied English drama and directing at
Columbia University and then served from 1953 to
1955 with the U.S. Army in Germany. He married
Helen Setzer in 1954.

Doctorow might well have gone back to graduate studies under the G. I. Bill, but he struck
out on his own, earning a living as an "expert
reader" for film and television production compa-
nies in New York. It was exhausting piecework—a
book a day, seven days a week, with a twelve-
hundred-word synopsis-critique evaluating the
book's potential for the visual media. An informal
evaluation of a novel for Victor Weybright, the
editor-in-chief of the New American Library, led
Doctorow to be hired as an associate editor in 1959.
By 1964 he was a senior editor; he next became
editor-in-chief and then a vice-president at Dial
Press, where he remained until 1969. Since that
time he has held appointments as writer-in-
residence at Sarah Lawrence, the University of California at Irvine, the University of Utah, Princeton,
and the Yale School of Drama; presently he holds
the Lewis and Loretta Gluckman Chair of American Literature at New York University. Doctorow
speaks of his work in mass-market publishing as
politically and morally rewarding, not just a necessary evil: "You could feel good about the way
you made your living—reprinting a first novel
that nobody knew about, working on everything

from Ian Fleming to Shakespeare to books on astronomy and every other damned thing, and seeing these books go out with price tags of fifty or seventy-five cents. I felt very good."[8]

And after reading scores of feeble novels and screenplays while working for the film production outfit, Doctorow decided to try writing a novel: "I can lie better than these people,"[9] he told himself. And indeed he could. His vision of "what the West must really have been like," *Welcome to Hard Times,* was published in 1960; it not only attracted excellent reviews but also achieved a Hollywood movie sale. Doctorow was hooked by the muse, and yet his next novel, *Big as Life,* would not be published until 1966. It turned out to be a disappointing attempt at science fiction.

If Doctorow's first two novels were superficially genre pieces from different genres, both narratives were in essence the account of intrusions by monstrosities into the lives of ordinary people. In *Hard Times* a terrifying bad man suddenly appears in a frontier settlement, raping and murdering and burning with the ferocity of a demon conjured into this world from some adjacent kingdom of evil. *Big as Life* is the tale of a pair of humanoids thousands of meters tall who seem to have torn through the texture of their own space-time dimension and fallen into New York harbor. The collision of worlds would continue to inform Doctorow's novels. It is one of his most significant imaginative concerns.

Introduction

With *The Book of Daniel* in 1971 Doctorow tried yet another narrative form: the historical novel. Here he used the Rosenberg spy trial and executions of the early 1950s as the core of his tale. *The Book of Daniel* achieved an impressive response, seeming to catch up in microcosm America's involvement with Vietnam, the silent majority's response to the radical minority—nothing less than the spirit of the late 1960s. The novel was a book for its time, and Doctorow was heralded as one of the nation's most interesting imaginative presences.

Doctorow published the best-seller *Ragtime* in 1975, and its readers, professional and amateur, were as delighted by the reading of it as they were unsure of exactly what it was they were reading. *The Book of Daniel* had been obviously modeled on the Rosenberg case, although with some subtle and important alterations. *Ragtime* took far more liberties with history and identity, for in this novel Houdini and Henry Ford and J. P. Morgan and Emma Goldman and a half-dozen others in the cast speak, think, and interact in ways that have no verification in objective reality. Doctorow followed *Ragtime* with a play, *Drinks Before Dinner,* in 1978, and with the novel *Loon Lake* in 1980. *Lives of the Poets,* which consists of six stories and a novella, appeared in 1984, and his 1985 autobiographical novel, *World's Fair,* won the American Book Award. *Billy Bathgate* appeared in 1989 and won the National Book Critics Circle award for fiction. Each work marked a new departure, a fresh emphasis. Doctorow would always take significant risks.

For example, *Loon Lake* is unconventional, eerie, and charming—somewhat in the manner of *Ragtime*, while managing to be more than a mere recapitulation of the earlier novel's experiments. In the later novel Doctorow has gone much further with the sorts of variations, contradictions, and plays upon the "truth" in the narrative that one associates with James Joyce or Vladimir Nabokov.

Doctorow's art is a unique fusion of moral involvement and poetic transformation. Like Philip Roth, he is a fabulist with a lesson to teach about the kingdom of America and the century of American ascendancy. Like Norman Mailer and Joseph Heller, he is distrustful of and yet spellbound by the misuses of power. Like William Kennedy, another city boy with a fascination for gangsters, crime and atonement for crime compel his most sensitive attention. Like Nabokov, prose for prose's sake is an art worth a lifetime's devotion. And like Poe, Melville, Ambrose Bierce, and Faulkner, there is a gleam of the macabre in Doctorow's created kingdoms—an unsettling taste for terror and blood. Leslie Fiedler once pointed out that there is a "disturbing relationship between our highest art and such lowbrow forms of horror pornography as the detective story, the pulp thriller, and the Superman comic book, all of which are . . . the heirs of the gothic."[11] In part,

Introduction

Doctorow is a gothic imagination in life-affirming America, and some crucial passages in his work are perhaps best read as "horror pornography." And it is important to remember that families and what happens to them lie at the marrow of almost all of his fiction.

Notes

1. Richard Trenner, ed., *E. L. Doctorow: Essays and Conversations* (Princeton, NJ: Ontario Review Press, 1983) 36.

2. Trenner 3.

3. Trenner 53.

4. Trenner 53.

5. Trenner 53.

6. *Lives of the Poets* (New York: Random House, 1984) 162.

7. "James Wright at Kenyon," *The Gettysburg Review* 3-1 (Winter 1990) 11.

8. Trenner 32-33.

9. Trenner 34.

10. Trenner 37.

11. Leslie Fiedler, *Love and Death in the American Novel*, rev. ed. (New York: Stein and Day, 1966) 156.

CHAPTER ONE

Welcome to Hard Times

Welcome to Hard Times is first the story of a Western massacre, and then of the invention of an ad hoc "family" from the survivors of that massacre, and then of the re-creation of a tiny village from the ashes of its buildings, social relationships, and human needs. But then the novel suddenly becomes the story of the bloody annihilation of all those things. The good news the book sets out is that the human instinct for community can create near-miracles with the least promising of materials. But the bad news it presents even more emphatically is that love and family and the circle of human society are not only far less powerful than the human instinct toward violence and revenge; they also seem to invite from out of the blue a ferocity that destroys them. This pessimistic formulation is characteristic of Doctorow and animates almost all of his fiction.

The novel is not only the story of the literal destruction of the village, Hard Times, in the Dakota Territory, but also the destruction of the animating dream that made its creation possible. It is thus a novel telling of the rebirth of a dream and then the destruction of that dream. It is also at heart a "city" novel set in the deepest Western wilderness, and one that champions the values of civilization against the savage energies of the countryside. This is a rare formulation in American fiction. From *Huckleberry Finn* through *Deliverance*, from *The Deerslayer* and *Sister Carrie* to *Bright Lights, Big City* and *Less than Zero*, American fiction usually assumes that the city corrupts while the country purifies. F. Scott Fitzgerald once observed in his private journals that "the cleverly expressed opposite of any widely accepted idea is worth a fortune to somebody."[1] If *Welcome to Hard Times* did not quite bring a fortune to its creator, it was an auspicious beginning for Doctorow's writing career, with the freshness of that beginning derived from cleverly expressing the opposite of one of our abiding national sentiments. The fortune would come later.

Doctorow's opening strokes are spellbinding: an enormous and sinister Bad Man from Bodie fills the bar at the Silver Sun with his wordless menace; he knocks back half a bottle of rot-gut just to clear the prairie dust from his throat, and then—literally the bodice-ripper—exposes to the men huddled at the bar the breasts of a redheaded saloon whore named Florence.

In a few moments Florence will be raped and dead; in a few paragraphs four men will die and the town be burned to the ground and a bloody revenge plot set into motion. The novel is a Western, but one very far from the heroic mode made famous by Owen Wister, Mayne Reid, or Louis L'Amour. Doctorow admitted to an interviewer that he enjoyed taking "disreputable genre materials and doing something serious with them,"[2] and his opening in *Hard Times* is an example of his predilection for packaging the serious inside the sensational. From the first sentences of his first published novel in 1960 on through the melodrama of *Billy Bathgate* almost three decades later, Doctorow has been a melodramatic writer. The reader should never ignore those self-proclaimed *disreputable* genre energies that animate his work from just below its surface. It is a quality essential to his appeal and his uniqueness.

The Bad Man from Bodie, Clay Turner, is more of an ogre than a human being, and Doctorow's account of the devastation he wreaks suggests some mythic violence from the bottom edge of nightmare. For a day and a night and another day the tiny frontier hamlet is transformed into a scene out of hell. Turner rapes, kills, and burns with abandon, and the delight he takes in destruction is demonic. Turner gleefully kills horses and men; he burns the flesh from the back of Molly Riordan, the town's other prostitute; he makes an orphan of Jimmy Fee, the scrawny twelve-year-old son of a carpenter foolish enough to try to fight back against the monster.

Understanding E. L. Doctorow

The first chapter of *Welcome to Hard Times* surges with a violence that will irresistibly breed its own counterviolence, for Molly and Jimmy Fee will not only eventually destroy the Bad Man, they will, almost literally, *become* him by the end of the book. Unlike genre Westerns, Doctorow's novel is not the simple tale of the triumph of good over evil; quite otherwise.

And if Molly and Jimmy are going to be transformed into murderers by the end of the account, the narrator of the tale, a widowed, thoughtful drifter in his late forties called Blue, can only watch, endure, and despise himself for his own cowardice in the face of the Bad Man's ferocity. Doctorow's revisionist Western is narrated by a gentle and ineffectual wordsmith at first too frightened to fight back. But the results of this departure from genre type are impressive, for the success of the novel resides more in its forlorn, overcivilized narrative voice than in its dramatic activity. *Hard Times* is a Western told as an Eastern. In an interview Doctorow speaks of the myth of the West as a creation of writers "having nothing to do with realities" and of his novel as a conscious "counterpoint to that."[3] By having his narrator *afraid*, Doctorow endows his narrative with a psychological authority genre fiction can never achieve.

For example, Doctorow creates an indelible image of the humiliation of failed male nerves: "Right then my hand began to move and I meant for it to go for my gun," Blue relates as he describes how he funks his opportunity to kill Turner at the bar. "But it went instead for the glass on the bar; I felt at that moment that I wanted to please him."[4]

It is also important to note that, in fashioning his demon, Doctorow recognizes that in creating menace out of mere words, less is always more. To give a local habitation and a name to the terrifying is inevitably to trivialize it, to dissolve the magic terrors of the glimpsed and the guessed in the universal solvent of everyday reality. As Leslie Fiedler once put it, "The abominable, to be truly effective, must remain literally unspeakable."[5] Clay Turner, the Bad Man from Bodie, hardly speaks a word, has no past, is explained by no psychological program. He simply *is*.

After the Bad Man has devastated the town and vanished back into the hills, Blue takes on himself the obligation of putting his little corner of the world back together again. He cannot help himself, for Doctorow indicates that Blue's impulse to rebuild a micro-civilization in the blackened emptiness of the Bad Man's carnage is nothing less than the essence of positive human instinct. Thus, the middle three-fifths of the novel is a tribute to the powers of human survival.

Blue uses half-broken tools, scraps of salvaged lumber, ceremony, words, love, and endless patience to reconstitute Hard Times out of its own debris and transform the fire-scarred prostitute Molly Riordan into his own wife and the orphaned

Jimmy Fee into his own son. "A person cannot live without looking for good signs, you just cannot do it," he tells himself as he labors to keep the flimsy town alive in the vast, merciless wasteland of the Dakota Territory. "And if I felt like believing we were growing into a true family that was alright: if a good sign is so important you can just as soon make one up and fool yourself that way" (89).

For a time Blue succeeds, and his luck runs strong. A cheerful, cynical Russian whoremaster called Zar arrives in town, and his two women draw some miners and their gold dust down out of the gaunt mountains that surround the place. A ne'er-do-well called Leo Jenks turns out to be a miraculous rifleman who hunts game for the entire community. Water trickles from a windmill-powered well. A Vermonter called Isaac Maple wanders into the scene looking for his brother, and Blue talks him into staying in Hard Times and setting up a dry-goods store. John Bear, a deaf and dumb Pawnee Indian, serves as the hamlet's physician and shaman. Blue gathers signatures for the petition for statehood, and capitalism personified as mining-company officials with spotless derbies and soft white hands consider Hard Times as the site of a road to their new stamping mill. The Dakota winter does not quite manage to kill the citizens of Hard Times, and the stir of spring life offers a promise that has little to do with reason and everything to do with the primal human impulse to connect life to life with bonds of ceremony, symbolism, word. "Molly was right, I would welcome an outlaw if he rode in. I felt anyone new helped bury the past" (124). Nothing should be excluded: *Welcome* to Hard Times. The achievement of so much "civilization" triggers in Blue the last refinement of the impulse toward civilization: the writing of history.

Using three big legal ledgers, Blue begins to chronicle all the human events in the village. The impulse to fix reality by scratching words onto paper is for Blue, and for Doctorow standing just behind Blue, spellbinding and ironic and necessary. And utterly futile. This paradox will appear again and again in Doctorow's work. The power and momentum of the real world cannot be captured in a writer's words, but the writer cannot resist the impulse to try to make that capture. Blue will realize at the novel's climax the pitiful irony of believing in the magic power of words, "as if notations in a ledger can fix life, as if some marks in a book can control things" (187). Still, mortally wounded by a shotgun blast, up to the last moment before his death Blue will scratch down his account of the violent cycle of evil and retribution-for-evil and transformation-into-evil that constitutes the real history of Hard Times. Writing is his duty and his fate. It is also his folly.

Doctorow is a novelist fascinated by families, and the bitterest irony in the novel's last movement concerns the failure of Blue, Molly, and Jimmy to transform themselves into the "true family" that Blue hoped they would become. For a long while Blue believes that Molly is simply schooling Jimmy Fee in the skills of Western manhood as she encourages their friend Jenks to teach the boy how to shoot; and Blue assumes that since he has legally married Molly and adopted Jimmy as his own son—affixed the three of them together with words on paper—the boy will forgo his revenge on the man who killed his real father. But the novel's dark climax is achieved out of Molly's and Jimmy's desperate need for revenge on the Bad Man from Bodie.

The mining company betrays Hard Times by deciding not to build its road through to the stripped-off mountain lodes, and in the midst of the village's financial death throes Clay Turner, the Bad Man from Bodie, returns to destroy again what the townspeople have so precariously restored. Zar and a Swedish prospector are killed in the ensuing gunfight. But Blue and the others are ready with an ambush this time; they have created a snare of barbed wire and lure the Bad Man into it. Trapped in the snare and nearly insensible from bullet wounds and a clubbing with a rifle stock, the Bad Man is helpless before Molly's avenging knife strokes. Blue cannot even specify her horrid deed, and his anguish is compounded by his realization of what her example does to Jimmy. "I cannot describe what she was doing, God have mercy on her, I saw the boy's horror, for how many endless moments did he endure it?" (212).

Welcome to Hard Times

Jimmy can only end Turner's agony and extinguish the horrific vision of Molly torturing him with her knife by destroying the man with a shotgun blast; Blue's left hand is shattered as he tries to deflect the shot that kills the woman and Turner. Dying, Blue can still write down the words that have always held him in thrall, and the novel's last and shortest chapter spirals out into a sort of existential oblivion: "Nothing is ever buried, the earth rolls in its tracks, it never goes anywhere, it never changes. . . . Why does there have to be promise before destruction?" (214).

Blue thinks at the last that he should perhaps set fire to the buildings of the town and allow cleansing fire to consume the half-dozen corpses now attended only by the Swede's mad wife and the "jackals and vultures, flies, bugs, mice" (213). The aftermath of the tragedy should at least be erased. But even this minimal dignity will be denied them all, for Blue realizes that creating such a funeral pyre is beyond his strength in the few moments left to him. And there is a sort of dismal natural economy he realizes he can still serve by abstaining from torching the dead husk of the town: "I keep thinking someone will come by sometime who will want to use the wood" (215).

Humiliated by his powerlessness in the face of Molly's and Jimmy's vengeful passion, and resigned at last to his own meaningless death, Blue's final entries in the ledger are simply words—his gift, his obsession, his folly. And here in *Welcome to Hard Times* it is important to comprehend the importance of Doctorow's preoccupation with the surrogate family of Blue, Molly, and Jimmy Fee. The family in collision with the world is Doctorow's most significant theme.

Critical esteem for *Welcome to Hard Times* has remained high for thirty years. Of all Doctorow's novels to date, it has excited the longest loyalties and the least dissent. On the novel's publication in 1960, Wirt Williams in *The New York Times Book Review* called it "taut and dramatic and exciting," and he called attention to Doctorow's imaginative handling of what Williams calls "one of the favorite problems of philosophers: the relationship of man and evil."[6] He went on to compare the novel to Joseph Conrad's *Heart of Darkness:* "When the rational controls that order man's existence slacken, destruction comes. Conrad said it best . . . but Mr. Doctorow has said it impressively."

Doctorow's philosophical subtlety gave his book a greater depth and staying power than the genre Westerns it contravened, and yet his tale is no less action-filled and vivid. But perhaps more importantly, his presentation of the West-winning epoch of the American adventure as animated more by greed, brutality, and anti-Indian racism than pioneer heroics has suited the temper of our times. When the novel was reissued in 1975, Kevin Starr called it "a superb piece of fiction: lean and mean, and thematically significant," and noted that Doctorow had purposely worked up nothing less than an "anti-western," taking the "thin, somewhat sordid and incipiently depressing materials of the Great Plains experience and fashioning them into a myth of good and evil."[7]

Similarly, the novelist Anthony Burgess found himself rereading *Welcome to Hard Times* after the 1975 publication of *Ragtime* and finding that the earlier novel was perhaps a superior book. The critic David Emblidge sounded a kindred note, looking back from *Ragtime* at *Welcome to Hard Times* and *The Book of Daniel* and claiming that both of the earlier novels "may in some respects be better pieces of fiction."[8]

Few critics have dismissed Doctorow's first novel, although Stephen L. Tanner has argued that *Welcome to Hard Times*, created by a man "living most of his life in New York City," is at heart a city man's failure to perceive the "pleasure, beauty, and spiritual invigoration that the Westerner's direct contact with a vast natural environment can produce."[9] The novel will certainly never please propagandists for the wide open spaces and apologists for the national West-winning myth. But at the very least, Doctorow must be allowed his vision and his premise. These are antiheroic times, and revisionist treatments of the West from Evan S. Connell's 1984 study of General Custer, *Son of the Morning Star*, to Larry McMurtry's 1985 novel, *Lonesome Dove*, to Kevin Costner's 1990 film, *Dances with Wolves*, have won critical esteem. Doctorow's dark fable remains one of the first and best attempts to show that the history beneath American history is worth a writer's most sensitive and intelligent skepticism.

Notes

1. F. Scott Fitzgerald, *The Last Tycoon*, ed. Edmund Wilson (New York: Scribner's 1970) 160.

2. Richard Trenner, ed., *E. L. Doctorow, Essays and Conversations* (Princeton, NJ: Ontario Review Press, 1983) 36.

3. Kay Bonetti, "An Interview with E. L. Doctorow," audiocassette recorded Feb. 1990 (Columbia, MO: American Audio Prose Library).

4. Doctorow, *Welcome to Hard Times* (New York: Bantam, 1976) 18. Further references will be noted parenthetically.

5. Leslie Fiedler, *Love and Death in the American Novel*, rev. ed. (New York: Stein and Day, 1966) 135.

6. Wirt Williams, "Bad Man from Bodie," *New York Times Book Review* 25 Sept. 1960: 51.

7. Kevin Starr, "*Welcome to Hard Times*," *The New Republic* 6 Sept. 1975: 25, 27.

8. David Emblidge, "Marching Backward into the Future: Progress as Illusion in Doctorow's Novels," *Southwest Review* (Autumn 1977): 397.

9. Stephen Tanner, "Rage and Order in Doctorow's *Welcome to Hard Times*," *South Dakota Review* 22 (1984): 84.

CHAPTER TWO

Big as Life

Big as Life, Doctorow's second novel, begins with a stoke of pure science fiction: two humanlike creatures thousands of meters high simply appear in New York Harbor from a space–time continuum adjacent to our own. But once Doctorow has this magical event in place and has introduced his cast of characters, he falters badly, failing to either frighten or fascinate the reader. "Unquestionably, it's the worst I've done," Doctorow has said of *Big as Life*. "I think about going back and redoing it some day, but the whole experience was so unhappy, both the writing and the publishing of it, that maybe I never will."[1]

Doctorow does have a story to tell, and one that most science fiction and fantasy writers might consider a promising variation on the invasion-from-space motif originated by H. G. Wells in *The War of the Worlds* (1898). But unlike a good adaptation of the Wells original, such as John Wyndham's *Day of the Triffids* (1951), Doctorow does not discover a way to employ the legacy of Wells's epic. *Big as Life* is a disappointment. This disappointment seems to stem from two sources, one of them mechanical and inherent in Doctorow's choice of story idea, one more subtly bound into his own artistic sensibility.

The mechanical problem with which Doctorow has stymied his novel concerns the attributes he gives his giants and the space–time kingdom from which they have appeared. The giants (a male and a female, and so an Adam and Eve from another space–time kingdom) are helpless—and almost motionless—in this local universe. They have fallen through some sort of cosmic scrim into this world, but the scale of time in which they are still imprisoned is not a terrestrial scale of time. Although humanlike in almost every respect, the creatures are not only thousands of times larger than earthly things but thousands of times *slower*. A single heartbeat requires about three and three-quarters of an hour. A jet airliner crashes into Adam's temple as the narrative begins, but his instinctive reflex to touch the point of impact will not be completed until the next midsummer and his cry of pain will not be heard for months. Earthlings can build scaffolding on the creatures, scheme to derive electricity for the Manhattan circuits from their body heat, probe or drill or explore their persons in unendangered leisure. Unlike Swift's Lilliputians, Doctorow's terrestrials have no need to tie down the intrusive giants from beyond the horizon. These Gullivers cannot threaten life here on earth because they are immobilized by the glacial time scale in which they are still encased. The giants are not threats; they are fossils.

But this immobilization makes for grave difficulties in creating a science fiction narrative. Wells's *The War of the Worlds* narrates the interplanetary battle between species with the stakes nothing less than survival or extinction, and his novel is filled with heroic action and relentless terror. Doctorow has nothing comparable to offer, and his tale languishes in consequence. The more subtle problem that disables *Big as Life* as a novel is Doctorow's failure to find an adequate means of expressing the fate of a human family in its clash with the world that always surrounds and threatens it, his abiding emotional theme.

The plot of *Big as Life* is less complex than that of *Welcome to Hard Times*, although both novels are of about equal length. In *Big as Life* Doctorow centers his attention on a free-spirited Manhattan jazz musician named Red Bloom and Red's girlfriend, a naïve Indiana farm girl called Sugarbush (her given name is Susan), and on a middle-aged bachelor historian named Wallace Creighton who becomes their friend. These three will come to be the novel's pseudo-family just as Blue, Molly, and Jimmy Fee constituted the pseudo-family in *Welcome to Hard Times*. Red and Sugarbush are sympathetic and intriguing characters, the book's only real successes (even though Doctorow cannot find for them enough to do), but Creighton seems a character still in search of his narrative and will have to wait until he is reincarnated as Daniel Isaacson in *The Book of Daniel* to achieve significance as a fictional sensibility. And although Red and Sugarbush are an attractive couple, sensual and life-affirming, this science fiction novel is not their proper milieu. The demands of the genre do not suit Doctorow's thematic and emotional concerns.

Doctorow has spoken of his affection for generating the premises of his books out of "disreputable genre materials" like the Western and science fiction. But *Big as Life* is neither a melodrama of pure genre adventure like Wells's *War of the Worlds,* nor does it manage to become the only other true alternative for the invasion novel type: an instructive fable in which human nature is illuminated by inhuman events, like George Orwell's *1984,* Pierre Boule's *Planet of the Apes,* Robert Heinlein's *Stranger in a Strange Land,* or E. M. Forster's little-known novella of future shock, *The Machine Stops.* Doctorow does not seem to be comfortable with a tale in which the amusement must necessarily lie merely in either external action or didactic uplift.

The appearance of the colossi in New York Harbor of course creates a crisis in world history, and America responds with the creation of a sinister superbureau, NYCRAD, the New York Com-

mand for Research and Defense. NYCRAD is
naked authority using the materialization of the
giants to justify the insertion of its tentacles into
every fiber of American life. The critic Arthur
Saltzman calls NYCRAD "Doctorow's version of
Big Brother,"[2] a good description of the new para-
government. The action played out in the balance
of the book is largely the story of NYCRAD versus
the human beings it has been created to protect—
Animal Farm with a touch of *Blade Runner*, perhaps,
with an attempted portrait of America in the grasp
of a right-wing insurgency that fails to be either a
warning, a prophecy, or a satire, although it fitfully displays elements of all three modes. Doctorow cannot seem to discover what sort of book
he is trying to write, and again and again the
reader is alerted for scenes and situations which
are promised and then anticlimactically withdrawn.

For example, it is apparent that Doctorow
once planned to have NYCRAD destroy the giants,
or at least that is the sort of inference the reader
is bound to make after watching the author's
scientist-politicians calculate method after method
for abolishing the humanoids rather than trying
to establish psychic contact with them. The novel's fourth and final part is even called "Practi-
cal Systems, Destruction," because the American
military-industrial mentality mirrors the mass
wishes of the American public, and the public
seems to want the extinction of the giants. If the
American man in the street fears the giants out

of superstitious awe, the American man in the uniform desires to destroy whatever can be destroyed because that is his nature. Even the scientific community succumbs to a panicky desire to rid the world of Adam and Eve rather than try to establish contact with them, for Doctorow's version of the American man in the laboratory fears that the giants might yet adapt to the time scheme of this universe and suddenly become aware of humankind, with catastrophic consequences; so contingency plans for the destruction and disposal of the giants are energetically prepared. Spouting Pentagon clichés, Doctorow's most ominous creation, a physicist named J. G. Putnam, coldly itemizes to Creighton seventeen different schemes that can be actuated to destroy the giants, which the scientists view a cosmic nuisance. And of course there is the possibility that perhaps those colossal organisms might already be breeding a disease against which humanity will have no medical defense. But Doctorow's book peters out before any of these dramatic possibilities can be realized, and his attempt to write a science fiction novel in *Big as Life* remains only a good, germinating idea—the colossi from an adjacent space-time warp—without an adequate plot to dramatize the implications. Still, even if the book has few intrinsic rewards, it now and again anticipates the successes that Doctorow will achieve in the next phase of his career.

For example, Wallace Creighton, the dusty-dry Greenwich Village historian who serves as this novel's man of words, appeals to the reader in his dismay, his honesty, and his affection for Red and Sugarbush. "I make fake what is genuine; most of my knowledge is secondhand," he tells the couple with disarming humility, and he compares their grace and charm as survivors amidst the hysteria and bigotry of a frightened city to figures out of the old William Powell Thin Man movies. No doubt speaking for his creator, Creighton states that the problem of the intellectual in America is that of impotence mixed with envy: "Our great generic failing is that we have no power"— an insight that Doctorow will dramatize in his more successful work. But although Creighton realizes that he has a priceless opportunity to write the history of a new order of human experience, Doctorow does not find his way into this opportunity, and he cannot integrate Creighton into the book's texture as he integrates Blue into the workings of *Welcome to Hard Times* or Daniel Isaacson into *The Book of Daniel*. Nor does Doctorow do much better with the narrative opportunities he has created for his various men of action to impose order after the appearance of the colossi. His sententious, senile General Hugh D. Rockelmayer never becomes much more than a parody of Douglas MacArthur, and his smiling opportunist of a think-tank scientist, Putnam, never puts any of his destructive programs into effect. Both these threads of subplot lead nowhere.

Even worse is Doctorow's failure to come through with a military-governmental conspiracy, for other than order some inoculations to be given to the populace and arrest random looters, the military government of Manhattan is clownishly ineffectual. Worst of all, perhaps, the closest thing to a good, scary chase scene in the novel occurs when Red gets himself capsized by a riot-control firehose and then manages to escape from the "comic skids and flops and cries of the involuntary vaudevillians" and find his way back to his pregnant wife. The Bad Man from Bodie in *Welcome to Hard Times* was an eerie and effective creation, but Doctorow's science fiction novel lacks all sense of immediate physical menace, a crippling deficiency in terms of narrative involvement.

But perhaps even more subtly crippling for *Big as Life* is the clash between Doctorow's liberal political sensibility and the intrinsic political implications of the invasion-type narrative. As far as it is valid to generalize about the tendency of certain sorts of imaginations to find appeal in certain sorts of narrative structures, it seems useful to suggest that the invasion narrative (or its generic cousins, the postnuclear narrative and the Robinson Crusoe narrative) tends toward a decidedly reactionary value system: it tends to become a narrative about the conditions of survival, and so inevitably a narrative about the survival of the fittest. Jack

Big as Life

London's *The Iron Heel* (1907), Ursula K. LeGuin's *The Left Hand of Darkness* (1969), Neville Shute's *On the Beach* (1957), William Golding's *Lord of the Flies* (1955), and the Mad Max films starring Mel Gibson made during the 1980s furnish instances of this predilection, and *The War of the Worlds* is the most famous instance of the type. *Big as Life* is not the novel in which Doctorow finds the formula that can embody his unique imaginative concerns. That fusion of voice, politics, and point of view will have to wait until *The Book of Daniel*.

Notes

1. Richard Trenner, ed., *E. L. Doctorow: Essays and Conversations*, (Princeton, NJ: Ontario Review Press, 1983) 37.
2. Trenner 83.

CHAPTER THREE

The Book of Daniel

Speaking of *The Book of Daniel,* Doctorow's 1971 adaptation of the Rosenberg espionage affair, the author told Paul Levine that his most difficult struggle with the material was the discovery of the proper voice in which to tell the tale. Doctorow had done part of a draft of the book "more or less as a standard, past tense, third person novel, very chronologically scrupulous." But reading back over the 150 pages of manuscript, Doctorow confessed that "I was terribly bored. That was a moment of great despair in my life, because I thought that if I could really destroy a momentous subject like this, then I had no right to be a writer. That moment, when I threw out those pages and hit bottom, was when I became reckless enough to find the voice of the book, which was Daniel."[1]

Readers seem to respond to novels in terms of structure, incident, moral and emotional identity with the players, perhaps charm of style as long as that style is not too eccentric. But writers must discover the proper voice for their story. "Each book comes in its own voice, not mine," Doctorow said to Kay Bonetti in an interview.[2] The problem is in *finding* that voice.

Doctorow's first two novels had been more or less conventional in terms of narrative tone and sequence of event. Moral discriminations, descriptive passages, scene connections, causes conducting to effects were all in place. But clearly this procedure would not do for *Daniel,* and Doctorow in desperation (and "desperation is the basic condition of writing," Doctorow has said) somehow found himself imagining the story being told via a narrative of images that simply appeared and accumulated before the mind's eye like photographs without captions, or video clips without any sort of voice-over commentary that would help the reader place the material in time, place, or consciousness.

The novel that resulted is a sort of prose video that takes place inside several consciousnesses, skipping at will from mind to mind, tone to tone, point of view to point of view. It became a modernist work, then, by virtue of its replacement of captions with pictures. Robert M. Adams has noted that T. S. Eliot's *The Waste Land* took leave of the stultifying conventions of the nineteenth century by "cutting off the horizontal decorative flow from image to image, in abrogating the familiar alliance of description and moral reflection."[3] Doctorow is a beneficiary of that departure.

Doctorow was not being facetious when he revealed to Larry McCaffery that a device inspired by commercial television had freed him from the incubus of his creative block. "You remember that television show *Laugh-In?* That was the big hit on television when I was writing *Daniel*. I told people when *Daniel* was published that it was constructed like *Laugh-In*. They thought I was not serious. But the idea of discontinuity and black-outs and running changes on voice and character—it was that kind of nerve energy I was looking for."[4]

The result of Doctorow's experiment with that narrational "nerve energy" is impressive: Daniel Isaacson, the son of parents electrocuted for treason against the United States, is the central consciousness of the tale, but by no means the only consciousness, and by no means will Doctorow make himself obliged to any spirit of consistency. The first few pages of the novel are a microcosm of its variousness and its extreme self-consciousness, its recognition of itself as an act of narrative. It is Memorial Day, 1967. A young man of twenty-five whose name seems to be Daniel Lewin (it was once Daniel Isaacson and perhaps will be again), his nineteen-year-old wife, Phyllis, and their eight-month-old son in a sling carrier are hitchhiking from New York City to Massachusetts. They are decked out in the costumes and insignia of what was known then as the counterculture: Daniel in John Lennon wire-frame glasses and a blue prison jacket ("cool, deliberately cool"), Phyllis in flower bellbottoms, with her long blonde hair in braids. The presentation is third-person omniscient. The reader is so far interested, amused, but hardly mystified.

And yet no sooner has this picture been set out than a first-person countervoice intrudes into the novel, preempting the narrative. Suddenly an intrusive, nervous "I" speaks directly to the reader, and this "I" is also a Daniel; and with his very first words this other Daniel chooses to write about his writing apparatus—*literally* about his writing apparatus: "This is a Thinline felt tip marker, black. This is Composition Notebook 79C made in the U.S.A. by Long Island Paper Products, Inc. This is Daniel trying one of the dark coves of the Browsing Room. . . . I feel encouraged to go on."[5]

The effect of the oscillation between these two points of view is of a consciousness so overcharged with nervous energy as to be jumping out of its skin, and this is exactly the effect Doctorow seems to want to achieve. Daniel is Hamlet: ghost-driven, half-nauseated, violent, desperately obliged to those on the other side of the grave, and yet feeling himself unequal to the task. And the novel will have its Ophelia, too.

The overvoice Daniel, the Daniel of the dark coves of the reading room, immediately shares with the reader his life concerns; some terrible news has last night been telephoned to him at his New York apartment to set in motion his family's hitchhiking journey up to Worcester. And yet Daniel seems compelled to tell us that the terrible phone call, laden with potential heartbreak and patently a scene from which any writer could create sympathy, had caught him in *flagrante delicto* in the midst of a sort of marital rape of his weeping, humiliated wife ("soft Phyllis from Brooklyn suffering yet another penetration and her tormentor Daniel gently squeezing handfuls of soft ass"[17]). The reader then learns that Daniel has been summoned to the site of his sister's suicide attempt. Susan, a grieving young Radcliffe Ophelia, had tried to kill herself with a razor blade in the restroom of a turnpike Howard Johnson's. Instead of the soft pastels of sentimental fiction, Daniel is presenting hard-edged, intimate prose photography.

Not only is the reader invited to be a voyeur in relation to these intimacies, but he is also half-seriously asked to commiserate with Daniel's writerly problems, too: "And if the first glimpse people have of me is this, how do I establish sympathy? If I want to show disaster striking at a moment that brings least credit to me, why not begin with the stacks, searching, too late, for a thesis?" (16-17). The book refuses to follow narrative expectations. The risks are enormous. But so will be the rewards.

Thus, the reasonable world of the library and all that it implies is invaded by the fantastic and forbidden. And this will be Doctorow's technique throughout. Sometimes it is 1967, sometimes the early 1950s, sometimes the Depression. The scene is now Cold War America, now Czarist Russia; the setting shifts instantly from Massachusetts asylum to California Disneyland to Bronx schoolyard. With stroboscopic speed the novel takes the reader into the minds of Daniel the graduate student and then Daniel the child and then Daniel the sexual "tormentor" and then Daniel the social theorist and then Daniel the grieving brother, and other Daniels besides. The reader is inside the minds of Paul and Rochelle, the accused, and briefly even in the mind of their lawyer. There are lectures about the dirty little secrets of American history. There are poems, slogans, political insights. Doctorow informs the reader of the significance of a given society's preferences in capital punishment, and there is a bizarre motif, part lecture and part magic incantation, that celebrates the deadly power of electricity. The reader is told of Daniel's biblical namesake, of his role as interpreter of dreams for "the dumb king, Nebuchadnezzar" (21), of his ability to survive in the lion's den, metaphors for the prophetic-seer role of Daniel Isaacson, who sees into the secret nighttime mind of the dangerous kingdom that has destroyed his parents.

In a fine passage that anticipates the method of interior monologue that he will develop in *Ragtime*—that is, the method of presenting a character's thoughts with an honesty and eloquence that character would not have been capable of without the aid of the author—the reader is taken by Daniel/Doctorow into the mind of the ghost of

Daniel's grandmother. She whispers to him from beyond the grave that her daughter Rochelle and her granddaughter Susan will end badly, for "they inherit from me, as you do, that excess of passion that shimmering fullness of stored life which always marks the victim" (82).

There is a brilliant, funny, politically doctrinaire description of the totalitarian meaning of Disneyland and Anaheim, California ("a town somewhere between Buchenwald and Belsen"), a set-piece introduced into the book solely because the opportunity intrigued the social theorist in Doctorow, for it makes no contribution to the plot: "In a forthcoming time of highly governed masses in an overpopulated world, this technique [of abbreviated shorthand culture for the masses] may be extremely useful both as a substitute for education and, eventually, as a substitute for experience" (305).

It was the modernist legacy of Joyce and Eliot and Woolf to have dissolved the walls of time, place, and identity, and in this novel those freedoms are exploited by Doctorow. But he is also free of any single tone and sense of decorum, perhaps an even more significant liberation for his sensibility. A rowdy, nervous, intimate, bizarre overvoice is the result. "I suppose you think I can't do the electrocution," Daniel/Doctorow whispers to us. Then: "I know there is a you. There has always been a you. YOU: I will show you that I can do the electrocution" (312).

And he does.

It is a memorable performance, experimental without being arty, liberated without being affected. Nothing exactly like it really existed in American prose before this novel. Doctorow recalls that his decision to speak through Daniel and to have Daniel speak through other sensibilities involved an exhilarating sensation of escape, and that his departure from the traditional conventions and covenants of the writer-reader relationship was like magic: "I sat down and put a piece of paper in the typewriter and started to write with a certain freedom and irresponsibility, and it turned out Daniel was talking, and he was sitting in the library at Columbia, and I had my book."[6]

Daniel's voice is the central nervous system of that book, and, something new in Doctorow's career, it is also a Jewish voice. Speaking in general of Jewish writers, the critic Mark Shechner says that "as immigrant, emigre, displaced person, or holder of dual citizenship, the Jew finds the correct interpretation of foreign signs a vital part of his daily routine, and has been obliged historically to turn the hyphen in his identity into the cutting edge of a sharp sensibility. . . . Amphibians that they are, Jews are experts in incongruity."[7] Certainly Daniel (Doctorow) is such an "expert in incongruity," for the reader is never to forget that for any Jewish imagination living in the post-Holocaust age there is an incongruity so large and terrible that the mind can hardly surround it, and that is the fact of Auschwitz.

Creating an experience of Jewish vulnerability and Establishment malice is central to Doctorow's artistic design, for in this novel his America is a kingdom of police and pogrom. Just as the blacks Coalhouse Walker and his wife Sarah will be the racial victims in *Ragtime*, so Doctorow's Jews are selected out for destruction here. Doctorow is a novelist of victimhood, *family* victimhood. By selecting as his central characters two Jewish parents and their children who *really were* a family hunted down by the state, Doctorow might be said to have attempted to create an American *Diary of Anne Frank*.

For example, as his parents await arrest and trial, Daniel (at about the age of nine or ten) projects the situation as might an American Anne Frank. It is Doctorow's brilliance to know just the properties that an American boy's mind would use to image the approach of this ultimate terror:

> All my senses are in a state of magnification. I hang around the house feeling the different lights of the day. I drink the air. I taste the food I eat. Every moment of my waking life is intensified and I know exactly what is happening. A giant eye machine, like the mysterious black apparatus at the Hayden Planetarium with the two diving helmet heads and the black rivets and its insect legs, is turning its planetary beam slowly in our

direction. And that is what is bringing on the dark skies and the cold weather. And when it reaches us, like the prison searchlight in the Nazi concentration camp, it will stop. And we will be pinned, like the lady jammed through the schoolyard fence with her blood mixed with the milk and broken bottles. And our blood will hurt as if it had glass in it. And it will be hot in that beam and our house will smell and smoke and turn brown at the edges and flare up in a great, sucking floop of flame.

And that is exactly what happens. (122)

In his autobiographical novel *World's Fair*, Doctorow wrote of the *real* woman killed against the schoolyard fence by an automobile and of her blood mixing with milk, one clue among many that the Rosenberg story allowed him to exploit his own childhood for the image system at the core of the book. This novel can then best be read as the effect of outward catastrophic events on the inward, tympanic sensibility of a child. It marks a great advance in Doctorow's achievement, for in neither *Welcome to Hard Times* nor *Big as Life* was he able to bring to bear on his creations his own identity and that primitive sense of black magic that really does characterize the distortions and magnifications of a child's mind. His first two novels were not really written from the inside. *The Book of Daniel* is almost nothing *but* inside: soliloquy, interior monologue, incantation, dream, speculation, prophecy. There is really little plot and almost no real reportage, no new *information*.

Notice, for example, in the passage quoted above, that the reader recognizes from his or her own experience the accuracy with which Doctorow captures Daniel's childish confusion of cause and effect. Daniel believes that the weather is controlled by primal black magic, directed against himself. But is this not *our* first belief—and a belief that, in the final analysis, no amount of reasonable and "mature" comprehension can ever quite extinguish? It is never wise to be too reasonable in describing imaginative art.

Although his prose is in this instance rather purple, the critic Gilbert Murray might almost have been anticipating Doctorow's third novel when he said that at the marrow of the most enduring stories there will always be

> a strange, unanalyzed vibration . . . an undercurrent of desires and fears and passions, long slumbering and yet eternally familiar, which have for thousands of years lain near the root of our most intimate emotions and been wrought into the fabric of our most magical dreams. How far into past ages this stream may reach back, I dare not even surmise; but it seems as if the power of stirring it or moving with it were one of the last secrets of genius.[8]

Thus, these primal "vibrations" reach the reader from out of Daniel's voice, sometimes overtly, sometimes subliminally. And the effect is of a strange and singular music. Daniel's voice is also the voice of his times: the Vietnam generation, the generation of *Sgt. Pepper* and the moon landings and the Chicago Ten and Charles Manson and Haight-Asbury LSD and Kent State and Malcolm X and Flower Power and the Watergate scandals and Black Is Beautiful, a generation that seems characterized everywhere by the slogans and symbols of upheaval, by its frank, jovial, self-congratulatory rejection of every sort of established authority. F. Scott Fitzgerald observed that a real generation can occur only about three times in a century, because a real generation involves a fundamental revolt against the fathers.

As a portrait of that generation's intellectuals and students, Doctorow's novel has turned out to have precision and staying power. This is an achievement of some magnitude, for it is always a difficult task to fix the identity of an era. The late 1960s were curious and, in the national experience, perhaps unexampled. Doctorow had to capture a complex self-consciousness, at once tender, narcissistic, and ironic.

The Vietnam generation defined itself by assuming a stance of profound revulsion with all adult authority and the American WASP establishment, a stance that twenty years of hindsight indicates was both theatrical and real in about equal measure. For it is only fair to remember that, compared to the near-universal suffering engendered by the American Civil War or the Great Depression just preceding the Second World War, the Vietnam generation hardly suffered at all—that it was to be a generation united by an attitude and a style that they had *chosen* for themselves, for they were not transformed into a generation in the crucible of catastrophe. Peace was indeed a cause. But it was also a costume.

"I hated the peace bandwagon worse than I hated the war," John Updike (Doctorow's exact contemporary) has one of his fictional alter egos declare. "It was a moral form of war profiteering. . . . All the fat cats and parasites of the system poor Johnson was sweating to save . . . the college boys, the bored housewives, the professors and ministers and the princelings of computer technology . . . freedom's just another word for nothin' else to do."[9]

Doctorow's Daniel Isaacson is the essence of his campus generation's dismay and distrust, but in Daniel there is no reaching for theatrical effect and no radical rhetoric for its own sake. He is alienated from the American WASP establishment because the establishment had one summer's midnight strapped each of his parents into the chair at Sing Sing penitentiary and killed them with bolts of electricity. Daniel does not *play* at alienation and radical campus theatrics, and his disquiet with the American national myth is desperately real. His sister Susan is driven into catatonia and finally suicide right before his eyes. For both the Isaacson children, childhood's worst nightmare has crossed over into reality to possess them. Obviously Doctorow's use of politics is crucial to the novel, for *The Book of Daniel* demands that the reader respond to it as a political tract as well as private description of experience. The novel is unabashedly a work of Leftist propaganda, as highly charged with moral outrage as George Orwell's *Animal Farm* and as anxious to reshape the reader's relationship to American historical pretensions as Thoreau's *Walden*, John Dos Passos's *U.S.A.*, or Joseph Heller's *Catch-22*.

"I was angry," Doctorow said in an interview. "It seems to me certainly a message of the twentieth century that people have a great deal to fear from their own governments. That's an inescapable world-wide fact. Daniel has a line about every citizen being the enemy of his own country. It is the nature of the governing mind to treat as adversary the people being governed."[10]

In *The Book of Daniel* the reader must once more attend to Doctorow's use of the family as the center of his drama. "The relationship between radical movements of one generation and another" was one of the key facets of the core idea of the novel, Doctorow told McCaffery. "The idea of a radical family—all the paradoxes and contradictions of that family against whom the entire antagonistic force of society is directed"[11] lay at the marrow of the book.

One of the most significant but little-remarked aspects of this novel is the fact that the historical

Rosenberg "radical family" was far more compromised than Doctorow's fictional Isaacsons. Doctorow wanted his family to be tragic martyrs to their own idealistic naïveté, to the political passion of their historical moment, to anti-Semitism, and to sheer bad luck. But in order to produce that effect he had to alter history and amputate biographical facts.

In the novel Paul and Rochelle are sent to their deaths by a slow-witted, frightened friend and former Communist party mate, the dentist Selig Mindish, who is being driven to confess by the pressure of FBI fabrication. Fearing deportation—his citizenship papers are not in order—Mindish is made to betray the Isaacsons as masterminds of a spy ring that furnished research secrets to the Soviets. In the novel there is no indication that the Soviets did not develop their own atomic power out of their own unaided research efforts: the Russian nuclear achievement may be simply an occasion for an American witchhunt and the Isaacsons sacrificial victims of our national paranoia. Mindish himself will serve ten years for his role in the spy operation. But of what crime are the Isaacsons guilty? And if they are not guilty, what crime is Mindish confessing to, and why?

Although it is never made entirely clear either to Daniel or to the reader, a tactical espionage substitution Doctorow calls "The Theory of the Other Couple" seems to be the device that leads to the execution of Paul and Rochelle, for in several

different ways the novel indicates that they are innocent, or almost innocent, of any complicity in
the theft and transmission of atomic research secrets. Daniel speculates that the Soviet spymasters
had allowed the FBI and the American justice system to arrest, try, and electrocute the innocent
Isaacsons to deflect attention from a *real* spy family
who resemble the Isaacsons in many particulars, a
family with two children who lived near the Isaacsons in the Bronx. In this version Mindish does
not betray the Isaacsons for his own safety; he sac-
rifices their lives and a decade of his own to allow
the Other Couple to escape. "They were about the
same age as my parents," Daniel tells Linda Mindish, the dentist's grown daughter, now caring for
her senile ex-convict father and practicing den-
tistry herself in Orange County, California. "To
protect another couple. . . . To keep the FBI away
from people of real value" (293-94) was perhaps
Mindish's motive, the Party's motive, the Soviets'
motive. How else explain Mindish's confession
and martyrdom?

But Selig Mindish is too far gone into senility
to confirm or deny Daniel's theory, and it remains
only the best guess as to why the Isaacsons were
betrayed. The old man spends his days enjoying
the high-tech attractions of Disneyland accompa-
nied by his aging wife, and Daniel will never know
the extent of his parents' complicity.

In historical reality, however, the Rosenbergs
were circumstantially far guiltier—or at least far

more guilty-*seeming*—than Doctorow's fictional analogues. Unlike Paul Isaacson, who is much too idealistic to compromise himself with war work for the plutocratic United States, Julius Rosenberg had worked for the U.S. Army Signal Corps in the creation of electronics designs for weapons and communications systems just before and during the Second World War. And the Rosenbergs were not destroyed by the manufactured testimony of a former friend like Mindish, who had no apparent access to significant research achievements. In the real trial Ethel Greenglass Rosenberg's brother, David Greenglass, gave the fatal testimony against them in exchange for his own life.

Doctorow has taken care to see that there is no figure in the novel equivalent to David Greenglass, for Greenglass had worked as a skilled machinist in the supersecret Manhattan Project in Los Alamos, New Mexico, and he was familiar with the design of the Nagasaki-type atomic bomb. Greenglass testified that the Rosenbergs were in charge of a spy network that had over the period of years conveyed key secrets of the Allied nuclear research effort to the Soviets and that his sister and brother-in-law had not only directed the operation but had recruited him into the ring. In historical reality, several figures suspected by the FBI of involvement in the nuclear espionage ring really did disappear forever as the first arrests were made, just like Doctorow's "Other Couple." By making his Isaacsons more innocent than were the Rosenbergs, Doctorow makes their children's plight more classically tragic.

Daniel is psychologically deformed by the weight and irony of this tragic burden, but his deformity allows him to bend and survive. Susan can only break. Dream-tormented Hamlet, flower-fragile Ophelia. The Daniel Doctorow presents is far from a passive sufferer or a one-dimensional martyr, nor is he anything like the usual sort of well-meaning boyish charmer that American writers from Twain to Fitzgerald to Philip Roth have made a significant feature of the national imaginative endowment. Daniel is not a companion, a champion, or anything resembling a saint. Daniel cannot *forgive*. It was Doctorow's discovery of Daniel's sensibility that made the novel possible, and it is Daniel in the grip of his demon-muse in his library carrel at Columbia who must empty the rage in his heart onto the page or be destroyed from within: write or die. Instead of the Ph.D. dissertation he pretends to be composing for the benefit of his wife and university—and a Ph.D. dissertation is at least in theory the very essence of civilized reason and responsibility—Daniel has created a sort of tortured prose soliloquy, haunting in its self-loathing, its cruelty, its startling, ugly honesty.

Daniel's personality is by turns vicious, vulgar, shocking, agonized. It is a sensibility funny, brutal, not quite sane—like the sensibility of a child. It is a portrait intimate and shocking and irresistibly readable. It is part grad student, part outlaw, part Hamlet. And yet it is also often a beneficiary of what Martin Green identified as "that idealistic eloquence about America which has been reborn in this century among intellectuals from newly immigrant families, and above all from New York Jews."[12] And yet it is part Lenny Bruce *schtick*, too: obscene, willful, anxiously perverse.

For example, in one of the most disagreeable scenes in contemporary American fiction, Daniel, returning by car to New York City from an emergency trip to try to help his sister survive a suicide attempt, makes a cruel use of electric fire against the world: he burns his young wife's bottom with an automobile cigarette lighter.

"Do you believe it?" Daniel queries the reader, mock outraged with the reader's voyeuristic participation in his viciousness—a voyeurism he knows perfectly well he has created and encouraged, an abomination he knows perfectly well he will be forgiven. "Shall I continue? Do you want to know the effect of three concentric circles of heating element glowing orange in a black night of rain upon the tender white girlflesh of my wife's ass? Who are you anyway? Who told you you could read this? Is nothing sacred?" (72).

In a memorable phrase T. S. Eliot described Hamlet's antic disposition as "less than madness, but more than feigned"—a caption that could be placed under almost any of Daniel's outrages. They are his means of maintaining a precarious sanity, a draining off of large evil done *to* him by means of a small evil done *by* him, and here the imagery of an electrical grounding strikes the reader as ironic and inevitable. To Daniel nothing *is* sacred. Incapable of this transmutation and soul purge, Susan is broken, catatonic, finally dead. She has the immaculate honor and yet the brittle vulnerability of the saint. Her brother holds that he and Linda Mindish are made of a different stuff than is Susan, a stuff soiled but unbreakable—that they will survive their humiliation and their tragedy by means of any device at hand:

> This is what happens to us, to the children of trials; our hearts run to cunning, our minds are sharp as claws. Such shrewdness has to be burned into the eye's soul, it is only formed in fire. There is no way in the world either [Linda or I] would be willing to use our sad lives; no betrayal impossible of our pain; no use too cheap of our patrimony. If Susan had only had a small portion! But nothing Susan did ever lacked innocence: no matter how loud, how demanding, how foolish, how self-destructive, nothing Susan did lacked innocence. (291)

In *Welcome to Hard Times*, Blue was a gentle man of words very much in love with the world he tries so poignantly to change. But Daniel Isaacson has no illusions about the world that has already done its worst to him. Doctorow was asked by an interviewer whether or not he had been tempted to make Daniel "a thoroughly sympathetic character, rather than giving him sadistic, at times almost monstrous, qualities." "Suffering doesn't make people virtuous, at least in my experience," Doctorow responded. "But I see his 'sadism,' as you call it, in a slightly different way. I see the scene where he abuses his wife, for instance, as the same kind of scene in which he throws his son up in the air. The act has existential dimensions. Daniel is over-tuned to the world. He doesn't miss a thing. He's a hero—or a criminal—of perception . . . [and he] survives by however cold and frightening embrace with the truth."[13]

It is important to notice that Daniel has been gravely wounded in his *family* feelings and that he lashes out at his wife, his child, his adoptive parents, and the sister with whom he shares his pain and humiliation precisely because they are family. For Doctorow, the violation of the family by the state is a near-mortal blow, a poisoned wound located just at the point of juncture where the individual personality, which cannot survive alone, draws its breath from the family that is, everywhere in Doctorow, its life-support system: "Of course, it would take a tremendous act of the will to accept the very idea of a family after this kind of thing has happened to you as a child,"[14] he told interviewer Larry McCaffery.

Susan, her creator feels, could only try to *limit* the truth she could handle, and the effort to reduce the dimensions of her tragedy is too much for her. She not only believes in the innocence of her parents, she believes that something must be forthcoming from the American national conscience in order to justify her parents' destruction, to compensate for their literal self-sacrifice. But the implications of her nation's act against her family are finally too much for her, and she becomes a proxy victim of the electric chair that killed them. Daniel must go on without her. But not alone.

If the political Right always promises to defend the family, the political Left always offers to furnish us a new one. This was the secret of the Left's appeal to the children of the American WASP and Jewish educated classes in the late 1960s. The movement perhaps succeeded in late-1960s America because it offered that sense of belonging which can only be derived from shared risks and shared adventure. However fatuous their rhetoric and naïve their political critique, the campus action groups instinctively comprehended the triviality of the bond that is supposed to hold together America's family life, and they moved to replace it with something stronger. The latter episodes of Doctorow's novel sketch this replacement.

Daniel's adoptive parents, law professor Richard Lewin and his wife Lise (living embodiments of the petty reasonable—humane, liberal, intelligent, "open," and so of course utterly incapable of dealing with the magnitude of Susan's and Daniel's tragic dismay) are straw figures pushed aside by glamorous guerrilla warriors of the Left.

In the depths of the Lower East Side, Daniel meets with such a guerrilla warrior, a "Digger" called Artie Sternlicht. They meet in order to discuss the founding of a "foundation for revolution" in memory of Daniel's parents' martyrdom and funded by their blood money (nothing comes of this scheme: one of the novel's many blind-alley subplots). Sternlicht is gallantly suffering through a bout of hepatitis contracted when the police blackmailed him into taking a blood test with a dirty needle: "The best pigs are very creative," he tells Daniel with cheery bravado and rueful admiration (148). Although a blood test is hardly routine in a political arrest, the cops had threatened to arrest Artie's girlfriend and stick her in a cell "with all bull dikes," unless he'd submit to a blood test, and of course all they really wanted was to infect him with some dangerous bacilli.

If Daniel is a Hamlet sicklied o'er with the pale cast of his own morbidity, Sternlicht is a Mercutio—witty, vulgar, brave, cynical, a man of intelligence and compassion who is also a man of action. Where Daniel loathes the world, Sternlicht loves it—and so of course would love to change it. "Peace marches are for the middle class to get its rocks off," he cheerfully tells a reporter from *Cosmopolitan* in front of Daniel and his own friends. "The peace movement is part of the war. Heads or tails it's the same coin. The Indian or the buffalo, it's the same fucking nickel. Right? And they're both extinct" (150).

According to Sternlicht, America needs to be
genetically altered with a radiation of images. And
the revolution America needs to undergo is a sort
of image revolution in its frontal lobes: "You don't
preach," Sternlicht tells Daniel. "You don't talk
about poverty and injustice and imperialism and
racism. That's like trying to make people read
Shakespeare, it can't be done" (154). Sternlicht realizes that the new post-McLuhan revolutionary
will make his revolution with images, and his medium will be that uniquely American art form, the
television commercial:

> That is today's school, man. . . . Commercials are
> learning units. . . . Hit and run. You got forty sec-
> onds, man. The media need material? Give them
> material. Like Abbie says, anyone who does any-
> thing in this country is a celebrity. Do something
> and be a celebrity. . . . We're gonna levitate the
> Pentagon by prayer and incantation and blowing
> horns and throwing magic invisibilities at the Pen-
> tagon walls. . . . We're gonna overthrow the
> United States with images! (155)

Whatever political optimism the novel contains is centered in Sternlicht's insights, and it is
no accident that, awakened and convinced by the
radical's vivacity and intelligence, Daniel is for a
moment able to halt the deadly progress of the
morbidity that is destroying him from within.
Daniel "suddenly sees the Lower East Side with
Sternlicht's vision: It is a hatchery, a fish and wild-

life preserve'' (154). The novel closes with the student closing of Butler Library at Columbia, the first famous act of the Movement and a media event par excellence. Doctorow's tone is not at all satirical or disillusioned with this act of imagery committed against the establishment by the student Left—far from it. ''Close the book, man,'' one of the SDS types tells Daniel. ''What's the matter with you, don't you know you're liberated?'' (318).

Liberated by images. In America, the kingdom of images. Doctorow would come to write his next novel out of that very concept.

Notes

1. Richard Trenner, ed., *E. L. Doctorow: Essays and Conversations* (Princeton, NJ: Ontario Review Press, 1983) 62.

2. Kay Bonetti, ''An Interview with E. L. Doctorow,'' audiocassette recorded Feb. 1990 (Columbia, MO: American Audio Prose Library).

3. Robert M. Adams, ''Precipitating Eliot,'' *Eliot in His Time,* ed. A. Walton Litz (Princeton: Princeton University Press, 1973) 139.

4. Trenner 41.

5. Doctorow, *The Book of Daniel* (New York: Random House, 1971) 13. Further references will be noted parenthetically.

6. Trenner 62.

7. Mark Shechner, ''Jewish Writers,'' *The Harvard Guide to Contemporary American Writing,* ed. Daniel Hoffman (Cambridge, MA: Harvard University Press, 1979) 220.

8. Gilbert Murray, ''Literature as Revelation,'' *Essays and Addresses* (London: Allen and Unwin, 1921) 244.

Understanding E. L. Doctorow

9. John Updike, *A Month of Sundays* (New York: Random House, 1974) 107.

10. Trenner 46.

11. Trenner 46.

12. Martin Green, *Re-Appraisals* (New York: Norton, 1967) 25.

13. Trenner 46-47.

14. Trenner 47.

CHAPTER FOUR

Ragtime

It is one measure of the singularity of *Ragtime* that it can be described as being at the same time a tragicomical novel starring American historical personages and also a sort of prose cartoon strip starring allegorical Everypeople purposely drained of biographical reality—a novel that is at once history, cartoon, political fable, and fairy tale. Some of the novel's events took place historically and some merely ought to have. Some of its events are painfully real and some of its events are charmingly magical. The tone in which the novel is told is sardonic and urbane and directed along a privileged wavelength of attitude and allusion, and yet the prose itself is intentionally flattened, declarative, chilly. Doctorow called the voice he used "mock historical-pedantic," and Stanley Kauffmann observed that "the absence of quotation marks on direct dialogue gives the book the visual effect of a saga discovered, rather than of a novel written."[1] It is a prose that seems intentionally parodic of the eighth-grade American history textbook, but with a text the *real* textbooks would not tell. And yet if the purpose is didactic, the manner is playful, ironic, self-aware, and brushed with the supernatural.

Doctorow's central intention seems to be to depict the invasion, from below and within and without, of a smug and secure American WASP family, circa 1908–1015, a family which is a microcosm of American self-conception at about the turn of the century. The novel is indeed a family and national *Bildungsroman*—an account of the nature of the American national character and the transformation of its identity. Such an ambition in such a form struck some critics as pretentious.

For example, the reviewer for *Time*, R. Z. Sheppard, spoke irritably of Doctorow's narrative hybrid as an unsatisfactory mix of domestic comedy and cosmic portentiousness: "As if Clarence Day had written *Future Shock* into *Life with Father.* Doctorow's images and improvisations foreshadow the 20th century's coming preoccupation with scandal, psychoanalysis, solipsism, race, technology, power and megalomania."[2]

A more sympathetic response came from *The New York Times Book Review,* where George Stade described the novel's texture as "absorbing rather than annotating the images and rhythms of its subject, in measuring the shadows of myth cast by naturalistic detail, in rousing our senses and treating us to some serious fun."[3] *Ragtime* is indeed serious fun, perhaps one of the finest didactic novels written about the American experience. There is much to learn, and Doctorow realizes that a useful simplification is the best first step in teaching anything.

It is 1908, or thereabouts—Doctorow is not going to be pedantic and literal in his use of chronological sequences, or in fact with any other dimension of his novel. He has claimed that history belongs to the novelists and the poets rather than to the social scientist: "At least we admit that we lie."[4] At this moment in American history the President of the United States, Teddy Roosevelt, the Rough Rider, has just finished giving the monarchies of the Old World a lesson they will not soon forget at San Juan Hill in Cuba. Protestant Anglo-Saxon America has just annexed Hawaii and put down the Philippine insurrection, so the little brown brothers and sisters of the Third World have been instructed in just what is good for *them*, too. (When McKinley seized the Philippines, he wrote "there was nothing left us to do but to take them all and to educate the Filipinos and uplift and civilize and Christianize them, and by God's grace do the very best we could by them, as our fellow men for whom Christ also died."[5]) In 1908 the Wright brothers are only five years past running a bicycle shop in Dayton, Ohio, and it will be almost half a decade until the Panama Canal is completed and the Model T Ford mass produced at the great factory in River Rouge. In 1908 America is still a small town three thousand miles wide.

But of course there are masked tensions under the small-town surface. This is Doctorow's crucial point and the moral substance of his novel. In 1908 America was still pretending.

> "In normal lives," T. S. Eliot wrote, "misery is mostly concealed. . . . In the Puritan morality that I remember, it was tacitly assumed that if one was thrifty, enterprising, intelligent, practical and prudent in not violating social conventions, one ought to have a happy and 'successful' life. Failure was due to some weakness or perversity peculiar to the individual; but the decent man need have no nightmares."[6]

Doctorow's "decent man" is called only Father, and as the story opens he has succeeded in the business of life just as Ben Franklin and Thomas Edison and Abe Lincoln indicated a penniless young American male should succeed. In fact, in 1908 Father sounds like figment out of Horatio Alger's daydreams. Educated at Groton and Harvard for a leisured but empty life, Father was fortunately forced to become a self-made man when his own father's investments failed after the Civil War. Now he manufactures fireworks and flags and patriotic paraphernalia and has done so well at it that God has rewarded him with a gold watch chain across his vest, a good digestion, a substantial income and a fine New Rochelle house, and a "large blond" wife and a son in sailor suit—in about that order of importance. He is a big-game hunter and an amateur explorer of real accomplishment, too, for the decent American man in the first decade of this century wants to be as much like Theodore Roosevelt as he can manage.

There is of course a Mother in the family, and Mother will learn a great deal about herself in the course of the action—revelations that will both startle and please. There is a maternal Grandfather in the family, too, about whom the reader never learns much other than that he is a sort of faded academic relic. There is the sailor-suited little boy of about nine or ten years, an artist-in-embryo (and perhaps an authentic clairvoyant) to whom no one but Doctorow and the reader pay the slightest attention. There is also Mother's Younger Brother living here in the big New Rochelle house, a moody, rudderless youth of perhaps eighteen in a white linen suit and a straw boater pining away for the infamous artist's model Evelyn Nesbit. The noted architect Stanford White has just been murdered for making Evelyn his mistress (an event that really transpired in 1906), and Mother's Younger Brother can think of no one other than Evelyn and schemes to have her for himself (and since Doctorow is writing a fairy tale as well as a history text, he will).

Nightmare genii are about to penetrate the shell of this smug American microcosm whose official belief is that "there were no Negroes. There were no immigrants."[7] After Doctorow gets through with it, America is not going to be able to pretend any more. By an accident that is not quite an accident, Harry Houdini, headlining in Manhattan, appears at the house one empty summer afternoon. This is wonderful. The little boy, like all little boys, is fascinated by the great escape artist's powers, and it is the first of the novel's magical events that Houdini's chauffeur-driven 45-horsepower Pope-Toledo auto just happens to break down in front of the house. Doctorow is setting in motion one of his most imaginative and intricate ghost machines. The car is only overheated, and while the chauffeur replenishes the radiator the magician spends a few moments in the family living room, just long enough to discover that Father has been chosen by Admiral Peary to join his third assault on the North Pole (an event that actually transpired in 1909).

The great magician Houdini will turn out to be one of Doctorow's most intriguing presences (he will also commandeer J. P. Morgan, Henry Ford, Sigmund Freud, and Emma Goldman, along other once-real people), and the author gives the reader a clue to the magician's profound self-contempt when we see that Houdini reacts with admiration to Father's Arctic adventure and dismisses his own feats of derring-do as just legerdemain to thrill children. "The real-world act was what got into the history books" (103), as he bitterly observes to himself later, when he has abandoned the real world altogether in pursuit of contact with his dead mother's ghost on the other side of death.

Just as Houdini is about to drive away from the New Rochelle house, Doctorow inserts into the scene a detail that will turn out later in this novel to be a clue that there is an organizing energy lying below the surface of the novel's world. It is the first instance of Doctorow's demonstration of a cosmic design beneath the outward, random look of things.

> The little boy had followed the magician to the street and now stood at the front of the Pope-Toledo gazing at the distorted macrocephalic image of himself in the shiny brass fitting of the headlight. Houdini thought the boy comely, fair like his mother, and tow-headed, but a little soft-looking. He leaned over the side door. Goodbye, Sonny, he said holding out his hand. Warn the Duke, the little boy said. Then he ran off. (11)

Almost halfway through the novel Houdini will have his chance to indeed "warn the Duke." Tragically, he will miss it. Houdini does not yet sense that the boy's words are an authentic signal to him from the Other Side, and the magician's recognition of their supernatural identity only comes much later and will even then be incomplete. And so the historical consequences of missing that signal from the beyond will be severe, for the Duke that the boy was urging him to warn turns out to be Archduke Franz Ferdinand, heir to

Understanding E. L. Doctorow

the Habsburg throne in Austro-Hungary, who will come to an airfield in Germany to witness with his "stupid, heavy-lidded eyes" (110) Houdini giving demonstrations of airplane flight for the Prussian military. If the Archduke could have avoided getting assassinated at Sarajevo on 28 June 1914, the course of world history would surely have been less tragic. But Houdini misses his cue, and the Duke is drawn along toward his own extinction and the flashpoint of historical catastrophe.

Doctorow is not quite done with this signal from the Other Kingdom, for in the novel's final pages we hear the little boy's warning from 1908 one last time. At almost the moment that the Archduke *really is* shot to death in the Balkans, Houdini is thrilling a Manhattan midday crowd with one of his most dangerous and audacious escapes. Dangling in a straitjacket upside down from a cable twelve stories over the pavement of Times Square, he undergoes "the one genuine mystical experience of his life":

> He was upside down over Broadway, the year was 1914, and the Archduke Franz Ferdinand was reported to have been assassinated. It was at this moment that an image composed itself in Houdini's mind. The image was of a small boy looking at himself in the shiny brass headlamp of an automobile. (330–31)

It was a swashbuckling turn toward narrative hyperconsciousness that rescued *The Book of Daniel* from the flatness that had so disappointed Doctorow in his first draft. Simple two-dimensional lifelikeness will no longer interest him as a writer, and he will never again construct a novel like *Welcome to Hard Times* or *Big as Life*. From *Daniel* on, his novels became acutely aware of themselves as artificial, self-referential texts. Here in *Ragtime* the author and the reader share an awareness of design and destiny of which the characters are only fitfully aware. A close look at some of the novel's small particulars reveals a tracery of coincidence, correspondence, and the supernatural surrounding its characters and events.

Thus, it is not really a coincidence that Mother has one of Emma Goldman's books on a woman's right to contraception on her bedside table, that Houdini glimpses Harry Thaw in his cell, that J. P. Morgan's library was designed by Stanford White. Or that Father and his little boy will in chapter 30 attend a New York Giants baseball game at the Polo Grounds and then that those very same Giants appear again in chapter 40, where they will infuriate J. P. Morgan as he emerges from the Great Pyramid after a harrowing night trying to communicate with primal energies from beyond death and finding his solitary vigil interrupted only by Egyptian bedbugs. These subtle tracings show the reader that although the purpose of Doctorow's tale is moral instruction, the technique of its telling is playful, ironic, multidimensional, as self-aware as a puzzle inviting us to solve it. Like

Joyce's *Ulysses* or Nabokov's *Pale Fire, Ragtime* is a novel which invites the reader to discern a pattern in its structure that its characters in their world of ink and paper cannot achieve the elevation to perceive. Close reading reveals that the entire circuit of characters in the book is linked with major or minor—in many cases minute—connections.

An example of a major connection, though still a connection that the characters involved do not themselves ever fully apprehend, is the linkage of coincidence which binds the New Rochelle family with two other families featured in the novel: those of the black musician Coalhouse Walker and his wife Sarah, and of the immigrant Jew Tateh and his never-named daughter. Myth and politics have seldom been so minutely interwoven, and the net of connections seems to vitalize the book's subsets of character and incident just as real nerves conduct impulses into living tissue. The circuit is detailed and elaborate.

Mother's Younger Brother ingratiates himself with Evelyn Nesbit and has a short, doomed love affair with her. She jilts him out of impatience with his devotion: "She loved him but she wanted someone who would treat her badly and whom she could treat badly" (93). Evelyn is almost always weak, greedy, exploitative in her relationships with the men who desire her so desperately, but there is one pure, passionate love in her that is wholly unselfish. This is her nonsexual fascination with a beautiful little Jewish girl. Evelyn falls in love with the girl, whom she glimpses in the Lower East Side streets on her chauffeur-driven way back from visiting in his Tombs jail cell her mad millionaire husband, Harry K. Thaw, awaiting trial (eventually dodging it by means of an insanity defense) for murdering Evelyn's lover, the architect Stanford White.

The nameless little girl's father is a destitute, Yiddish-speaking silhouette artist Doctorow will only call Tateh—Yiddish for "father"—who is identified thus as the ghetto analogue to the WASP Father of New Rochelle. Tateh, his rigid sexual puritanism outraged by the mere thought of the defilement, has just expelled forever from their tenement rooms his wife, Mameh, for daring to offer to sell herself as a prostitute to keep the three of them from starvation. He is half-mad with mourning (to him, his wife is dead), and frenzied with the consequences of his conscience. In analogy to the WASP Mother of New Rochelle adopting the black washergirl Sarah and *her* baby, Evelyn expresses some urgent, motherly love hunger in herself by befriending Tateh and his beautiful child. For a time Tateh tolerates her intrusion into their lives because of its benefits to his daughter, but he despises Evelyn as the most infamous sexual adventuress of the era—her picture is everywhere—and she recalls to him all too vividly his castoff wife's willingness to barter sex for bread: "My life is desecrated with whores," he tells her in Yiddish (61). He will not stand for it long.

Through her connection with Tateh and his daughter, Evelyn meets the historical anarchist Emma Goldman (Doctorow will show the reader the chain of linkages that will lead away from this meeting, too). But Tateh, anticipating with horror the inevitable brutalization of his child in the Manhattan slum jungle and fearing for her corruption at the hands of the infamous society whore Evelyn Nesbit, simply steals away one day with his daughter on a northbound trolley, no destination in mind and some thirty dollars hidden in his pockets and shoes.

If Doctorow rejoiced in exploiting what he called "disreputable genre materials" like the Western and science fiction for his first two novels, here in *Ragtime* it might be suspected that he is commandeering for his vehicle a creaking pushcart right out of Yiddish melodrama. After all, the situation could hardly be more charged with potentially mawkish sentiment: penniless immigrant father, immaculate lovely daughter, Lear and Cordelia as orphans of the storm. But Doctorow's storytelling powers make the situation work because he convinces us of its reality. "Nothing is as good at fiction as fiction," Doctorow observed for a symposium on the importance of fiction for *Esquire*. "It is the most ancient way of knowing but also the most modern, managing when it's done to burn all the functions of language back into powerful fused revelation. . . . You will experience love, if [fiction] so chooses, or starvation or drown-

ing or dropping through space or holding a hot
pistol in your hand with the police pounding at
the door. This is the way it is, it will say, this is
what it feels like."[8]

Doctorow does not hesitate to revise some history for political effect. But first he organizes his
episodes by means of synchronicity and magical
correspondence. This is the method with which he
links his forty short chapters and his half-dozen
subplots. At their transfer station in New Rochelle, Tateh and his daughter glimpse none other
than Mother and her sailor-suited little boy, and
the little girl seems to find some nameless magical
connection in the lad's face. But for the moment
nothing comes of her inarticulate apprehension of
the presence of fate.

Transferring again and again, Tateh and child
make their way by interurban trolley up into Massachusetts (total fare: $3.40), where Tateh finds
work at a factory woolen loom in Lawrence and se-
questers his daughter inside their unheated rooms
to keep her free of the world's vile touch. The immigrant factory workers, outraged by the exploita-
tions by the Lawrence textile concerns, initiate a
violent strike. (The real strike in Lawrence did not
occur until 1912, but the effect Doctorow knows he
can achieve is simply too good to miss). The Inter-
national Workers of the World sends its most char-
ismatic orator, the historical Big Bill Haywood, to
encourage the strikers, and Tateh, despite his fears
for his daughter's safety, finds himself committed

to the labor struggle out of admiration for the ag-
itator's eloquence. Tateh, beaten by the police
strikebreakers, manages to hoist himself onto the
departing child's train, and eventually he and the
girl end up in Philadelphia. "From this moment,
perhaps, Tateh began to conceive of his fate as separate from the fate of the working class" (137). For
$25 apiece he contracts to create for the Franklin
Novelty Company what they call "movie books"—
flip the edge of the book pages with your thumb
and a little one-reeler takes place before your eyes.

And so when next we see him fifteen chapters
later, Tateh has become that most fantastic of truly
American successes, the movie mogul complete
with jodhpurs and white linen cap, and that most
preposterous of truly American parodies, the er-
satz aristocrat complete with bogus title and fake
accent. No one unmasks him and the past does
not rise up to destroy his celluloid castle—far from
it. He has "invented" the move serial (Doctorow's
real father turned down a chance to star opposite
Pearl White in *The Perils of Pauline*, preferring to
keep his secure job in a bank, so this may well be
an instance of Doctorow's revenge on facts). And
Tateh has secured for his daughter a luxurious life
that perhaps will compensate for the expulsion of
her mother and the years of poverty. He will even
get to marry a lovely Christian woman and live
happily ever after—in Hollywood, of course.

Still, one interviewer was so disturbed by
Doctorow's failure to administer moral justice to

Tateh that he asked the writer if he had "been tempted to condemn [Tateh] for abandoning his working-class ideals." Doctorow's response to the query is revealing because it is so tough and unsentimental, and it is a response worth keeping in mind when the reader comes to assess the moral implications *Loon Lake* and *Billy Bathgate:*

> "No, I love that character, but also understand him," Doctorow replied. "I was making an observation in my treatment of him, that very often a man who begins as a radical somehow— with all his energy and spirit and intelligence and wit—by a slight change of course can use these gifts to succeed under the very system he's criticizing . . . As compassionate as we feel for Tateh and as much as we love him, here's a man who has betrayed his principles and sympathies and gotten ahead that way."[9]

By coincidence—always a highly charged term in *Ragtime*—Tateh, now calling himself Baron Ashkenazy, meets the New Rochelle family at the Jersey shore. Tateh's daughter and Mother's small, quiet son become inseparable on the beach, and "the Baron" charms the family, especially Mother, whose blond beauty intrigues him. History soon contrives to separate them all—even though history will eventually contrive to bring some of them back together. Father is called to New York to deal with Mother's Younger Brother's role in the occupation of the Morgan Library by Coalhouse Walker and his band. The morose young idealist has turned his passion for Evelyn Nesbit Thaw into a commitment to radical justice. He comes under the influence of the radical Emma Goldman, and his commitment to social transformation and his skill with anarchist explosives will eventually kill him.

And war is in the air, the Great War of 1914–1918. The ragtime era will end with a bang, not a whimper. The family does not quite comprehend why Fritz von Papen of the German army should be so interested in examining the particularities of the Jersey shoreline, but it is with foreshadowing details like this that Doctorow signals that the great catastrophe of the war will reach out to their lives quite shortly. Mother's Younger Brother will soon die with Zapata's peasant forces in the Mexican Revolution.

Father discovers that the young man's legacy to him includes blueprints for no fewer than seventeen ordnance devices of futuristic design, for Mother's Younger Brother turns out to have been a combination of Leonardo da Vinci and Tom Swift who had secretly created designs for grenade launchers, land mines, sonar-directed antisubmarine depth charges, infrared sights, and so on, weapons some of which are "so advanced that they were not used by the United States until World War II" (332). At once good American patriot and good American profiteer, Father converts his factories from fireworks to munitions in antic-

ipation of America's entry into the conflict and secretly conveys to both the American and Allied
high commands Mother's Younger Brother's astonishing blueprints for death. Father is himself killed
along with 1,194 others aboard the *Lusitania* on 7
May 1915, when the German submarine U-20
torpedoes the vessel off the coast of Ireland, the
episode which made inevitable America's involvement in the war. "Mother wore black for a year"
(333), and then Tateh, ingenuously revealing to
her that he is not a baron at all but a simply a very
rich Jewish socialist from Latvia, asks and receives
her hand in marriage.

Although the social convulsion which leads to
the occupation of the Morgan Library and a dozen
deaths originates in race hatred, and although the
novel offers no evidence at all that America can
solve its racial crisis (quite the contrary), Tateh,
the perfect American entrepreneur, extrapolates
from a idyllic scene just outside his window in
California the movie gimmick that will mark his
greatest success. "He suddenly had an idea for a
film. A bunch of children who were black and
white . . . little urchins who would have funny adventures in their own neighborhood, a society of
ragamuffins" (334).

Tateh is seeing, of course, *Our Gang*, one of
the gauziest American fantasies of them all, and
his vision of the commercial possibilities of this
happy racial detente forms an ironic coda to the

thematic burden of the novel, which indicates that America's racial crisis is deep and probably insoluble. The very existence of the "schwartze child" in Tateh's triptych is in fact one of the novel's most crucial plot devices and the fulcrum of its moral scheme. But to explain the significance of the child it is necessary to return all the way back to chapter 9. *Ragtime* is that kind of book.

While Father is gone on his expedition to the North Pole, Mother discovers in the family garden a living baby who turns out to be the illegitimate offspring of a neighborhood washergirl called Sarah and a black ragtime musician, Coalhouse Walker. Doctorow told an interviewer that he'd heard the true prototype of this story from his wife, and "I found myself using it in *Ragtime*, where I never knew in advance what was going to happen."[10]

What does happen sets in motion the entire march of events that forms the moral scheme of the novel. It is a tale of race and of property, those two enduring American obsessions. Coalhouse Walker, the musical gentleman "of color" whose refusal to be racially humiliated infuriates a certain sort of white ("he had created himself in the teeth of such feelings"), comes weekly to see his lover and the child he has sired. With each visit he passes the rowdy Irish crew of the Emerald Isle Engine Company of volunteer firemen. The sight of an uppity black man driving a Ford automobile through these lily-white precincts does not sit well with them. Pretending to be charging him a toll for the use of the road into New Rochelle, the firemen end up defiling and eventually destroying Coalhouse's car. He demands restoration or restitution. These are refused. Then Sarah is badly injured when she tries to reach the Republican candidate for vice-president, Sunny Jim Sherman, in order to ask him to intervene on her lover's behalf. One of Sherman's military bodyguard strikes her savagely with his rifle butt. When Sarah dies of pneumonia brought on by her injuries, Coalhouse sets out to exact a terrible vengeance on WASP America.

With dynamite and shotgun Coalhouse ambushes and assassinates a half-dozen of the racist firemen. Now the black man the press calls the "killer arsonist" lays siege to New York, murdering more firemen and taking for a hostage something far dearer to the white American's heart than the mere life of any of our citizens—property. In this case Coalhouse and his rebel band, the "Provisional American Government" (and we hear in our mind's ear echoes of the IRA's Provos), occupy and threaten to dynamite the collection of treasures Pierpont Morgan has accumulated in the marble library building he has caused to be erected as his own monument on 36th Street. Coalhouse's ordnance man is Mother's Younger Brother, lately the chief designer at his brother-in-law's fireworks factory, and with this defection compounding Mother's adoption of the black orphan child Doctorow signals that the smug WASP

New Rochelle Everyfamily of 1908, transformed by compassion and outrage, has been changed forever. This disillusion even includes that holiest sacrament of American life, business itself—for if, as Calvin Coolidge claimed, the business of America is business, even that central mystery is exposed "for the dreary unimaginative thing it was" when Mother commands for a time the family enterprises during Father's Arctic adventure.

The domestication of yesterday's radical visions is central to America's political evolution, Doctorow feels, citing as illustration for his claim the fact that Emma Goldman's outrageous proposal that abortion simply be made available to any woman who wanted it had become in the eight intervening decades since her deportation from these shores the orthodoxy of today.

In the Coalhouse Walker subplot of *Ragtime*, Doctorow has literalized this political insight. Radicalism is not only "part of the family"; it is the basis for the formation of the family—in this case, the radical family of ideology which inevitably replaces the feeble family of genes, habit, and decorum that is the American middle-class legacy, Eliot's "decent" life of gentility and inhibition. Mother's Younger Brother is simply Artie Sternlicht from *The Book of Daniel* writ large.

Realizing that he will inevitably be destroyed for his bloody vigilante presumption ("a ceremony of vengeance in the manner of the ancient warrior"), Coalhouse demands that the racist fire chief of the Emerald Isle company, Willie Conklin, be given over to him for blood justice. This is not done, nor does Coalhouse really expect it to be. Then Booker T. Washington, the living embodiment of social humility as the cost of economic advancement for the black race, meets with Coalhouse under the flag of truce and admonishes the revolutionary to see that his intransigent demand for revenge is dragging to their deaths the half-dozen young blacks and the young white man in blackface, Mother's Younger Brother, solely in order to satisfy the claims of his own vendetta.

In order to save his men, Coalhouse softens his demands to a simple and symbolic restoration of his automobile, for he will not give up his life without transforming its loss into a moral lesson about the rights of a black. Negotiations are completed, and fire chief Willie Conklin is made to assemble an entire Model T from its disparate parts at curbside in front of the Morgan Library. But of course Coalhouse and his men realize that the completion of the automobile will signal the musician's destruction, for at that moment he has promised to give himself up to the authorities. The grim climax of the novel occurs as Coalhouse is shot to death in the street by "a squad of New York's Finest armed with carbines" (315).

Behind the geniality of its temperament and the cheerful audacity of its method, the novel is surely a dark, violent prophecy from out of the age of which it is written to the era that will come to read it—our era.

For *Ragtime* Doctorow has invented a style which, by its seeming *negation* of style, manages to throw into relief the slightest nuance of irony he applies to character, episode, description. Without seeming effort the novel catches up on the quick-silver of its small, radically curved surface a micro-cosmal concentration of the American world during the first decade of our century, a world that convinces with the accuracy of its miniaturization and the authority of its dramatic metaphor. Doris Grumbach spoke for a number of American re-viewers when she praised Doctorow's "adroit clev-erness" in plotting and the subtle humor just beneath the simplicities of its "Dick-and-Jane-and-Spot prose." And like many of her colleagues in the American literary community, she saw nothing wrong with Doctorow's reinvention of historical incident as a technique to highlight the inner truth of the ragtime era, "the world of simplicity and op-timism at the turn of the century" when it might have still been possible for America "to make peace between classes and races in this country."[11]

Reviewers for such important publications as *The New York Times*, *The Village Voice*, *Newsweek*, *Saturday Review*, and *The New Yorker* awarded the novel high praise when it was brought out in 1975 and post-Vietnam America was in a revisionist mood. For example, George Stade claimed in *The*

New York Times Book Review that Doctorow had achieved an impressive breakthrough in his invention of a technique that could capture "the fictions and the realities of the era of ragtime."[12] Eliot Fremont-Smith said in *The Village Voice* that Doctorow's novel was "simply splendid" on one level and yet also "complicatedly splendid" in its deeper levels of meaning, implication, and irony, "a bag of riches, totally lucid and accessible, full of surprises, epiphanies, little time-bombs that alter one's view of things."[13] Writing on the novel for the *Washington Post*, Raymond Sokolov called it "brilliant and graceful" and said that it was Doctorow's marvelous trick to "throw the knowns and unknowns together in a racy plot that uses conventional history as its main premise and spins on outward from there in a zany extrapolation . . . [that turns] history into myth and myth into history."[14]

Even critics who disapproved of *Ragtime* as a pretentious fairy tale admired its animation and charm and conviction. For example, Hilton Kramer disliked Doctorow's Leftist political bias; *Ragtime*, he claimed, "distorts the actual materials of history with a fierce ideological arrogance." But Kramer praised the book's "delectable aesthetic surface."[15] Like many of his colleagues, Walter Clemons in *Newsweek* was pleased rather than disturbed by Doctorow's reinventions of episode and encounter, finding an exhilarating freedom in the book's presumption: "The demarcation between fiction and history is magically dissolved. . . . I found myself looking up details because I *wanted* them to be true. . . . The grace and surface vivacity of *Ragtime* make it enormous fun to read. But beneath its peppy, bracing rhythms sound the neat, sad waltz of *Gatsby* and the tunes of betrayed or disfigured promise that the best American novels play in one key or another."[16] And Stanley Kauffmann's response in *Saturday Review* was to praise the novel as an authentic modern masterpiece: "*Ragtime* is a unique and beautiful work of art about American destiny, built of fact and logical fantasy, governed by music heard and sensed, responsive to cinema both as method and historical datum. . . . Doctorow saw ways to fuse imagination with imaginatively dramatized history, to distill an era. . . . This book, any page of which may seem simple, is complex and rich."[17]

But the novelist's meddling with objective historical facts made several reviewers uneasy. They doubted that invented episodes were "truer" than the events fixed in historical reality. And perhaps because Doctorow had sheathed his radical politics and racial pessimism in just such a funny, deadpan, "pseudo-pedantic" style, in the manner of a book written for young adults, some critics reacted negatively. From the moment of its publication, *Ragtime* has provoked striking instances of critical dissent. It has proved to be Doctorow's most controversial book.

For example, in a review in *Commentary*, Hilton Kramer distrusted the message he felt was concealed beneath the novel's surface charm: "The stern realities of Mr. Doctorow's political romance—its sweeping indictment of American life, and its celebration of a radical alternative—are all refracted, as it were, in the quaint, chromatic glow of a Tiffany lamp, and are thus softened and made more decorative in the process."[18] Martin Green made a similar charge in a review in *The American Scholar*, accusing Doctorow of taking "gross liberties with history in the name of art" and of encouraging the reader to indulge himself in a radical chic daydream, "to give ourselves the airs of revolutionaries, in purely fantasy and wish-fulfillment conditions."[19] Writing in *The Atlantic*, Richard Todd called *Ragtime* "the most overrated book of the year"[20] largely because of what he found to be its simplistic political message. Predictably, the conservative *National Review* disliked the political bias of the novel, and even while praising Doctorow's "exquisite prose medium," Jeffrey Hart noticed that Doctorow played favorites with Coalhouse Walker and Emma Goldman: "Both of these characters are exempt from the moral skepticism in which Doctorow bathes his WASPs and his Irish. . . . The serious danger to Doctorow as an artist is thus sentimentality."[21]

Some British reviewers also objected to the Leftist radicalism and racial melodrama Doctorow built into his tale. Like the conservative American reviewers, they felt that Doctorow had attempted a serious political seduction under the cover of an appealing, pseudo-naïve narrative manner. Thus, Jonathan Raban conceded that *Ragtime* "is a consistently bright, thoroughly readable book," but he was annoyed by the political bias, by what he felt were its facile caricatures, by Doctorow's gleeful alterations of historical reality, and by the opportunistic relocation of the story from character to character, episode to episode. In Raban's final analysis the novel was "a cunning, fragile house of cards. Its major interest lies in the way in which it suggests a recipe for the contemporary bestseller. It is written to be read fast."[22]

Another British reviewer, Paul Levy, announced that he was speaking for "almost all British critics" and "several thousand common readers" when he sarcastically identified the *real* plot of *Ragtime* as its sales campaign, and claimed that Doctorow had failed to live up to the splendid promise of *The Book of Daniel*. Levy described *Ragtime*'s construction as "a little nostalgia here, a little noble left-wing sentiment there, and the lashing of semen whenever the reader's interest threatens to wane." He cited the author's alterations of history as its gravest fault and linked this sentimental falsification to the needs of "the book's natural constituency of trendies."[23]

It is likely that critical reaction to the book will continue to be divided along the issue of its political vision of America and, as one type of response to that vision, the right of an artist to alter and invent a fable "truer" than mere facts. As Roger Sale crystallized this phenomenon in *The New York Review of Books*, Doctorow's procedure was to lay out "impudently and gravely historical actions which did and didn't happen,"[24] and implicitly assert that his creations in *Ragtime* carried a poetic truth formerly concealed from us by our complacent allegiance to "mere" facts. Clearly, the fame and hype that surrounded the initial appearance of the novel were partly just a fad. But the novel that remains in the aftermath of the fad is an enduring achievement.

Notes

1. Stanley Kauffmann, "A Central Vision," *Saturday Review* 26 July 1975: 21.

2. R. Z. Sheppard, "The Music of Time," *Time* 14 July 1975: 64.

3. George Stade, *The New York Times Book Review* 6 July 1975: 1.

4. Richard Trenner, ed., *E. L. Doctorow: Essays and Conversations* (Princeton, N.J.: Ontario Review Press, 1983) 67.

5. Quoted in Alfred Kazin, *An American Procession* (New York: Knopf, 1984) 251.

6. T. S. Eliot, introduction, *Nightwood*, by Djuna Barnes (New York: New Directions, 1961) xv.

7. Doctorow, *Ragtime* (New York: Random House, 1975) 4, further references will be noted parenthetically.

8. Doctorow, "Ultimate Discourse," *Esquire* August 1986: 41.

9. Trenner 45.

10. Trenner 44.

11. Doris Grumbach, *The New Republic* 5, 12 July 1975: 31.

12. Stade 2.

13. Eliot Fremont-Smith, "Making Book," *The Village Voice* July 1975: 41.

14. Raymond Sokolov, *Book World* 13 July 1975: 3.

15. Hilton Kramer, "Political Romance," *Commentary* Oct. 1975: 79.

16. Walter Clemons, "Houdini, Meet Ferdinand," *Newsweek* 14 July 1975: 73, 76.

17. Kauffman, 20, 22.

18. Kramer 80.

19. Martin Green, "Nostalgia Politics," *American Scholar* 45 (Winter 1975/76): 843.

20. Richard Todd, *The Atlantic Monthly* Jan. 1976: 96.

21. Jeffrey Hart, "Doctorow Time," *National Review* 15 Aug. 1975: 893.

22. Jonathan Raban, "Easy Virtue: On Doctorow's *Ragtime*," *Encounter* (Feb. 1976): 74.

23. Paul Levy, "Historical Truth v. Fiction," *Books and Bookmen* 46 (June 1976): 21.

24. Roger Sale, "From Ragtime to Riches," *New York Review of Books* 7 Aug. 1975: 21.

CHAPTER FIVE

Loon Lake

L*oon Lake* is an audacious book in style and construction. The novel is sometimes moving, sometimes funny, usually interesting, but not always successful as drama or social critique or literary experiment, and not always conscientious in its craft, either. Anthony Burgess, a distinguished and innovative novelist himself, said with justice that the novel displayed "the admirable faults of the overreacher," and that if Doctorow had not quite brought off his effort, he had indeed made "a very honorable attempt at expanding the resources of the genre."[1] *Loon Lake* lacks the emotional focus of *The Book of Daniel;* nor does it manage to find a source of fascination equivalent to the cast of historical personalities Doctorow commandeered for *Ragtime.* And, just as with his 1989 crime saga *Billy Bathgate,* Doctorow seems to get tired of the novel nine-tenths of the way through and concludes his tale with a jarring mixture of exasperation, ad hoc invention, and fatigue.

Loon Lake is at once three kinds of book: a Depression-era *Bildungsroman;* a love-triangle thriller in the manner of, say, James M. Cain; and an ironic critique of that uniquely American symbiosis, capitalism wed to crime. There is a young man with a taste for adventure and there is a traveling carnival and there is decadent old money and there is ownership ruthlessly infiltrating a labor strike and there is a great deal of sex, some of it well described and erotic and some of it well-described and freakishly repulsive. If the structure suggests Nabokov, the content summons up Hemingway, Jack London, Upton Sinclair—and the Warner Brothers B-unit of Hollywood, California, circa 1936.

Loon Lake is something of a science fiction novel, too, at the level of its structure if not in its subject. *Big as Life* derives its shock value from incursion of giants from another space-time continuum breaking through into a world like this one, yet it is a tale still recognizably conventional in its narrative structure. *Loon Lake* offers a far more radical dislocation under its surface. Space and time and event inside it are multiple versions of "our" space and time and event. Things happen in *Loon Lake.* Then they happen again, but now only *almost* the same way that they happened before. And then different things happen altogether, with no final authority as to which event in which space-time continuum "really" takes place. Doctorow's world does not offer us an absolute standard by which to decide.

Doctorow begins his tale in the summer of 1936, the very depths of the Depression. A young street punk known only as Joe ("I stole what I needed and went after girls like prey") takes it on the lam from the blue-collar world of Paterson, New Jersey. His immigrant "hunkie" parents are dutifully working themselves to death for meager wages, a "lousy little house" on Mechanic Street, linoleum floors, radio shows, Mass, failed dreams. Joe wants to be free and, if he can manage it, he wants to be famous too. Protean of personality, Joe is hardly content with shoplifting, alley-stabbings with his penknife ("I stuck it in a feeb with a watermelon head"), robbing the poor box at church, discovering sex with a Grammercy Park housemaid. He knows he wants to be someone other than himself, but he cannot seem to find the final version of that other. Describing himself while attending the movies on the housemaid's money, "he fitted himself out in movie stars he discarded them."[2]

Joe feels that with each experience some "silent secret presence grew out to the edges of me" (8). The adult world may be hollow and pretending and afraid ("I understand the meagerness of the adult world"), but merely seeing through it is not enough. Joe will not be tamed by the respectable world, but he also must find out what he *is*, and so Doctorow sends him out into the vast forests of the North where invisible energies will guide him to his fate—and to himself.

In 1936 America was a kingdom of wheels: auto wheels, train wheels, the wheels of the carnival caravan. Homelessness was one side effect of the Depression, and in millions of lives motion became a substitute for meaning. Out on the open road Joe receives his political education from hobo socialists in random Hoovervilles ("it was a kind of music"), and then he catches on with Sim Hearn's carnival on its slow, sordid journey through the slag-gray villages of the Adirondacks. He has an affair with Sim's wife and then takes off. (Doctorow delays until much later in the novel some alternate-universe versions of Joe's affair with Sim's wife.)

In the depths of a midnight forest Joe experiences a vision "of incandescent splendor" (31), a private train car passing only a few yards from him and, within it, a beautiful naked blond girl trying on a dress. In his *Paris Review* interview, Doctorow said that this image of the young vagabond staring in amazement at the naked girl on the private train was the point of origin from which he subsequently imagined, backward and forward, the rest of the novel.[3]

Spellbound, Joe follows the tracks toward the major dramatic locus of the book, the thirty-thousand-acre hideaway of mysterious multimillionaire F. W. Bennett and the cast that surrounds him: the kept poet Warren Penfield, the kept woman Clara Lukács, the kept gangster Tommy Crapo, and much more—including, ultimately, the solution to the riddle of Joe's own identity. Although Doctorow is quick to point out that his own prose style is indebted to film for its scenic fluidity ("We've learned we don't have to explain things"[4]), he has borrowed from film something far more significant than its immediacy and its freedom from the need to explain. That is, the cast of *Loon Lake* seems to have been derived less from literary antecedents than from Hollywood celluloid. In fact, it seems fair to say that the Hollywood film of the 1930s is the inspiration of Doctorow's novel. The "disreputable genre material" around which he organizes his work is not the Western or the science fiction novel this time, as it was with *Welcome to Hard Times* and *Big as Life;* it is the Hollywood B movie.

But one would need to go outside the movies for the prototypes of a couple of Doctorow's characters. Most significantly, although her part in the novel is a mere cameo, Bennett's beautiful, patrician wife, the famous aviatrix Lucinda Bennett, is obviously modeled on the historical Amelia Earhart. Lucinda will even vanish mysteriously on a similar air voyage in the South Pacific in the same year, 1937, as did Earhart. It is the glamorous, striking, or tragic events of the 1930s that Doctorow uses for the background of his tale. This is crucial to the mental atmosphere of the story.

Understanding E. L. Doctorow

Because he was born in America in 1931, it would
be fair to suggest that Doctorow's first and perhaps deepest impressions of the great world beyond his corner of the Bronx would be just these
things. For all the modernity of its technique, the
strongest impression created by the book is one of
nostalgia for a period of glamour and excitement
that World War II and its Holocaust and nuclear
megadeath would forever trivialize. Doctorow is
writing a Depression novel about socialist vaga-
bonds and drunken poets who've given their
hearts away to dimestore floozies and glamour society wives dying in seaplane accidents, and these
are the anachronistic glamour properties of the
movies and radio shows and newspaper headlines
of his Depression boyhood, not of his wartime
youth or his Cold War college years. There is a
strong suggestion of *tribute* in *Loon Lake*—tribute
and a sort of imaginative recovery of a once-
glimpsed world not quite one's own. He does not
seem to revise history so much as recover it. Something like this recovery may well lie at the heart of
the impulse to write novels set in the recent past.
Indeed, for many people it is not the contemporary scene but the world just *before* one's own that
furnishes the heroic daydreams—that just-out-of-
reach world that technicolors one's childhood with
its heroic energies but will remain forever the
world we *just missed* living in.

Doctorow's novel gives off that sort of feeling,
a feeling found everywhere in it but which re-

mains difficult to localize and define. It does not seem farfetched to claim that only an imagination taking its impressions from the American movies of the 1930s or from the radio back in the days when the radio still told stories would produce this kind of tale. Confirmation for this argument occurs in Doctorow's autobiographical novel *World's Fair.*

Still, one of the biggest disappointments in *Loon Lake* is that, unlike the Hollywood hacks from whom Doctorow took his dramatis personae and the makings of his plot, Doctorow does not do enough with his materials. Injured by Bennett's guard dogs, Joe is mysteriously hired on as a gardener while he heals. When Clara decides to leave on the occasion of Lucinda Barrett's sudden return, Joe for some reason agrees to help her escape. They steal one of Bennett's cars, a 1933 Mercedes-Benz, and head off into the American landscape.

Although Joe has stolen an automobile and a mistress from a man of great ruthlessness and power, the young vagabond decides that he will follow to the end his lone-wolf code—"the toughest and most dangerous and the classiest thing" (180). He goes to work for Bennett yet once more, this time under a pseudonym as a production line worker at Bennett Autobody Number Six, Jacksontown, Indiana. Joe, now calling himself Joe Paterson, lives as if married to Clara in their company house on Railroad Street. Clara, only months before the gold digger par excellence, is supposed to find her cindery little bungalow adequate compensation for the loss of her sinecure in Bennett's Adirondack harem.

But improbable as this factory interlude is in terms of human psychology, these chapters do allow Doctorow the scope to generate some good effects, among them a memorable picture of life on the production line and a couple of the most convincing characters he has ever created, Lyle and Sandy James. The production-line set-piece is a dark experience conveyed to the reader by a witty, ironic style. Through the imaginative accuracy of his prose Doctorow manages to involve us in the apparatus of the American factory as it was back when the workers were just interchangeable parts. The peculiar despair of the sort of work that is Henry Ford's legacy to the modern world is well portrayed:

> High above my head the windows of the great shed hung open like bins and the sun came through the meshed glass already broken down, each element of light attached to its own atom of dust and there was no light except on the dust and between was black space, like the night around stars. Mr. Autobody Bennett was a big man who could do that to light, make the universe punch in like the rest of us. (187–88)

Noise, nerves, repetition, speed—again and again and again the same wires and screws

through the same holes, the human mind searching frantically for relief: *How do I get out of here?*

> And then I resolved not to think at all . . .
> knowing I couldn't feel hope in this hammering
> noise. But I didn't have to try not to think, by the
> middle of the afternoon my bones were vibrating
> like tuning forks. And so it had me, Bennett Au-
> tobody, just where it wanted me and I was
> screwed to the machines taking their form a mile
> away in the big shed, those black cars composed
> bit by bit from our life and the gift of opposition of
> thumb and forefinger, those precious vehicles,
> each one a hearse. (189)

Lyle and Sandy James are Doctorow's most interesting character creations in this book. Hillbil-
lies from the mountains of the South, the Jameses
are up here in "Mr. Autobody Bennett's" factory
attempting to make a living, and they dearly miss
their rustic home. Country innocence versus city
corruption is one of the most significant sets of op-
posing terms in the American imaginative heritage, and with impressive powers of observation
Doctorow brings the reader into the world of folk
from the hills turned into factory cannon fodder.
The portrait of these two brave, dispossessed
Southern souls is so subtle and accurate that it is a
keen disappointment when the reader discovers
that Lyle is an antiunion spy working for the
suave, labor-busting gangster Tommy Crapo, Bennett's chief enforcer and not so long ago Clara's

lover. Clara's past as Tommy's girlfriend rises up to reclaim her at the climax of Joe's portion of the novel and sets in motion the bizarre series of events that hastily conclude the tale.

"Good fiction is interested in the moral fate of its people," Doctorow has said.[5] That is an unarguable claim, but Joe of Paterson goes through such rapid and arbitrary moral metamorphoses in the concluding episodes of *Loon Lake* that it is difficult to have much confidence in his creator's conception of him at this point. Discovered as a management "mole" set in place to anticipate the union's strike plans, Lyle is killed in a snowy sandlot after being denounced as a Judas by some workers who had trusted him. Badly beaten and with his arm broken, Joe survives, but the police, complicit in management's scheme against the union, hold him for questioning. Joe extricates himself from what is beginning to look like a frame-up by claiming to be F. W. Bennett's son. He has in his wallet Bennett's unlisted phone number at Loon Lake and, even though he's stolen Bennett's Mercedes and girlfriend, demands that the police call the industrialist to confirm his paternity. Incredibly, the police release him when, on what one presumes to be an offstage call to Loon Lake, Bennett evidently confirms Joe's identity as his son. Meanwhile, Clara has been recognized by one of Tommy Crapo's operatives and she deserts Joe for the gangster without even a word of goodbye.

Having left his biological family back in New Jersey and then lost his pseudo-marriage to Clara, Joe now joins the rest of the Okie emigration along the snowy January wastes of Route 66 toward "the great honeypot of lower California." The fifteen-year-old widow and mother Sandy James is with him in his truck. They have become lovers, but Joe, like all Doctorow heroes, has an irresistible impulse toward familyhood, and she accepts his proposal of marriage as eagerly as Molly accepted Blue's in *Welcome to Hard Times*.

But in a kind of tragicomical parody of Joe's transforming vision of a nude and infinitely desirable Clara inside Bennett's private Pullman car, Sandy sees inside the passing Super Chief a gorgeous movie star whose name she can't quite remember, and Joe recalls himself from the proletarian prospects of his California future back toward the Gatsby-like dreams of himself that he'd had only months before. He realizes that he has traded some grand and mysterious birthright for a young widow and her baby and a future for himself as just one more anonymous clerk or factory hand. Fate in the form of a newspaper headline administers a death blow to his marriage plans. In a discarded rotogravure section of a Sunday paper a couple of weeks old, Joe finds pictures of Lucinda Bennett on what the headlines call HER LAST FLIGHT, and from the pictures he realizes that the unidentified man in those photos is Penfield, who has evidently perished with her when *The Loon* vanished into the Pacific somewhere between Hawaii and Japan.

Joe's response to this news is astonishing. And F. W. Bennett's response to Joe's response is more astonishing still. Abandoning his bride-to-be and her child sleeping in the train coach, Joe goes back to Loon Lake, where a grieving Bennett gives him Penfield's old room. Joe proceeds to absorb all the writings that the poet has left behind him. He then proceeds to *become* Penfield: "My life is your life" (130), Penfield had once prophetically told Joe when the poet had seen that Clara loved the newcomer. Now it has come to pass that, almost literally, their lives *are* one: "Perhaps we all reappear," Penfield had written to Joe in his last note before the fatal flight. "Perhaps all our lives are impositions one on another" (205).

Certainly Joe's is an imposition on F. W. Bennett's, for another and even more mysterious prophecy is fulfilled at Loon Lake. "I might be a Bennett son!" Joe had realized earlier, trying on clothes in front of Bennett's full-length mirror during his recuperative period after the dog attack. This was Gatsby's dream, of course: the essential American dream of creating ourselves from next to nothing, the self-fathering dream of the archetypal American who has only himself to thank for his own magnificent success. "And then I felt again my child's pretense that those two gray sticks in Paterson were not really my parents but my kidnappers! Who knew whose child I was!" (90).

From the moment of his return to Loon Lake, he is *literally* Bennett's child. Doctorow's fairy tale has at last come full circle. "Mourning had illuminated the natural drift of his life to isolation," Joe says of the grieving Bennett. And yet Bennett has enough room left in his heart not only to allow the young thief to live with him and listen to his reminiscences of Lucinda, but the industrialist will legally adopt Joe as well. For some reason Doctorow will even claim in the last hurried sentences of this novel that, when the Jacksontown police called Bennett to see if Joe was really his begotten son, Bennett had never received the call, or at least he has no memory of receiving it. Still, even if he had received the call, Bennett could have had no reason to have honored Joe's bizarre claim. And as for the Jacksontown police releasing him, Joe just shrugs at this improbability: "Perhaps there were moral operations in this world that transcended the individual responsible for them and threatened to ruin everyone. Was that it? Was I perceived as a leper who threatened to contaminate them?" (292). So much for official motivation.

But even though Joe now has the "terrible shame" of deserting Sandy and Baby Sandy, the young nobody from Paterson allows the vacuum of his identity to be filled with a manufactured new soul that is pure Bennett. Although everything in the novel up to this point indicates that Joe despises Bennett's politics and power ("a killer of poets and explorers . . . the outrageous absurdity of him was his power. . . . Oh my Clara I swear Mr. Penfield by the memory of the Fat Lady I know how to do it" [293]), what Joe swears by blood oath to do is not to destroy Bennett but to *save* him by "growing in his heart his heart bursting his son" (293).

The political revulsion and the lesson of the production line have utterly vanished. Joe accomplishes his transformation into a Bennett scion by casting off his initial New Jersey street-punk persona, and then casting off the Clara-lover persona, and then casting off the persona of the would-be husband of Sandy, and also casting off the newly acquired Penfield persona, and then evolving more or less instantaneously into the son that Bennett *ought* to have had. Henry James once spoke with disdain of the regrettable weakness of novelists of his era for " 'a happy ending,' or a distribution at the last of prizes, pensions, husbands, wives, babies, millions, appended paragraphs, and cheerful remarks." Doctorow is guilty of almost every count of that indictment.

Joe's original last name turns out to have been Korzeniowski, Joseph Conrad's real surname, which Doctorow impishly suggests he included "perhaps to confound the Ph.D.s."[6] And he has probably taken Clara's last name from George Lukács, the Hungarian literary theorist. Far too much can be made of this correspondence. Doctorow cheerfully admitted that he did not know what was going to happen in *Ragtime* when he sat down at the typewriter from one day to the next, and in *Loon Lake* that feeling of creation and countercreation for the sheer fun of it seems even more pronounced.

A mystical linkage of event that has come to be called "synchronicity" runs through *Loon Lake*, and in Joe's biographical entry we are not really surprised to discover that he was born on August 2 in 1918, for both F. W. Bennett and Warren Penfield, both of whose life lines intersect Joe's, were also born on the second day of August—Bennett in 1878, Penfield in 1899. Doctorow will force other synchronous events on his creation in the last page of the novel. Only a year after his stint as a roustabout for Sim Hearn's carnival and nine months after he had proposed to a fifteen-year-old widow amidst the Arizona tumbleweed, Bennett's brand-new son is in Williams College, lettering in blueblood sports like swimming and lacrosse. Joseph Paterson Bennett has a good World War, too, winning the Bronze Star for commando operations with the OSS in occupied France, then joining the CIA with the other tough upper-class Cold Warriors who gave that organization its unique tone. (Billy Bathgate will do almost the same sort of self-transformation with *his* patrimony in an ending equally unlikely.) Twice married, twice divorced, childless, the last one hears of Joe recalls the last one heard of Tateh: destiny triumphing over sociology. Joe belongs to Bennett's New York, Newport, and Saratoga clubs, and he is, like his adoptive father, the last Master of Loon Lake—arrogant and sterile, the perfect American captain of capital.

Although the novel has these startling "appended paragraphs" it is Doctorow's use of synchronicity that constitutes his most striking departure from the conventions of mainstream fiction.

Carl Jung is the intellectual presence most closely associated with the concept he termed "synchronicity," which is Greek for "simultaneousness." This term has come to indicate a connectedness between events that are separated in time and space. Appropriately, Jung himself is shown accompanying Freud on his New York visit in *Ragtime,* and he receives a most Jungian "shock of recognition, although at the moment he could not have explained why" (32) when he sees Tateh's daughter watching her father cut Evelyn Nesbit's silhouette, the first incarnation of the concept that Doctorow takes much further in *Loon Lake.*

A certain kind of contemporary writer delights in the opportunity to create a universe fraught with powers and crisscrossed with symmetries which the larger God or the larger Nature have absent-mindedly ignored. Robert Scholes called this sort of artist-with-words a "fabulator," and Joyce, Nabokov, Borges, Pynchon, Robert Coover, Günter Grass, and Donald Barthelme are the writers who have perhaps drawn the most attention toward this aspect of their work. Clearly,

Ragtime and *Loon Lake* are fabulations—narratives inside reimagined little universes of their own.

Warren Penfield's life is the major means by which Doctorow expresses this synchronicity. The reader finds Penfield's synchronicity almost always in conjunction with Joe's life, for the novel shows us now Warren's life, now Joe's, with images from one life hauntingly resembling images from the other, as if "bleeding" over from adjacent channels of electromagnetic transmission. And to make things even more complex, Doctorow will also change things *inside* each life, then superimpose *these* changes on each other. Thus, Warren seems to rise out of the electronic depths of Doctorow's computer, and before the poet is even properly introduced the reader sees him experiencing as a boy in Ludlow, Colorado, an image that is at once comical, beautiful, embarrassing, erotic (precisely the congeries of reactions Nabokov so often evoked): a beautiful infant girl being held out in the air by her mother and pissing "tulips" onto the Colorado dust (12). Late in the novel Joe is shown experiencing in New Jersey almost exactly that same vision; but now the little girl being held out to relieve herself is perhaps Clara ("I immediately recognized you Clara" [131]). As with the "Warn the Duke!" synchronicity and its recurrence in *Ragtime*, the little universe of Doctorow's novel is held together with such symmetries and mystical incursions from the beyond.

To follow the image chain of the pissing little girl, for example, it comes as no surprise that when Warren first sees Clara at Bennett's Adirondack retreat, he recognizes her and she, wordlessly as Tateh's daughter recognizing the little New Rochelle boy in *Ragtime*, responds to him, too, even risking her career as Bennett's favorite courtesan to sleep with him. "And so the recognition must be mutual and it pushes us toward each other," Warren muses (52), completing the thought that Carl Jung just missed making when he saw—and seemed to somehow recognize—Tateh's daughter in *Ragtime*.

It is Warren Penfield's fate to die not once but twice in air disasters with Lucinda Bennett, for there are two different versions of their last moments over the Pacific, two different versions of their Icarus-fall. There is no deciding which version is "real." The only valid response is: Both are.

In the first of these death scenes, the dipsomaniacal poet is for once not simply whining in "expressive self-magnifying complaint" but recalling for Lucinda his first sexual experience with the unnamed little immigrant girl in Colorado, and the reminiscence is interrupted by ominous dark Pacific thunderclouds: "It's nothing. A line squall" (37), Lucinda says as the scene goes to black like a film scene.

But later in the book Warren's tender reminiscence in the doomed airplane is of an anonymous street-sweeping Japanese girl fate had chosen for him when he was searching through Zen Buddhism to find his own identity. The Buddhist monastery is going to expel Warren for his liaison, and the lovers, sharing no more words than do Warren and the immigrant girl in the other, Colorado version, slip away to the anonymity of Tokyo. "I thought I could support us by teaching American customs and manners to Japanese businessmen" (140). But Doctorow the melodramatist makes this version of the tale into a variation on *Madama Butterfly*, and his agency of death is purest fate. The girl is killed along with about 140,000 others in the Tokyo earthquake of 1 September 1923.

This second scene cuts to black with the same ominous thunderheads, the same reckless dismissal by Lucinda: "It's nothing. A line squall." Both versions are of course completed by the newspaper headline—HER LAST FLIGHT—that fate leaves for Joe on the California-bound train. And both versions are equally real. Nor is Doctorow through with the Warren Penfield variations even now. In the last image flashes crowded in at the end of the book, there is yet a third version of the romantic tale.

In this version Warren disguises his child bride as a boy. On the slope of a mountain he creates a magic powder that changes his young lover into a giantess, and he rushes into her vulva to "continue my lifelong search for the godhead" (291). Warren's body shrinks to microscopic size, then expands upward and outward with the absurd instantaneousness of the dream, cracking the girl open "like an egg."

But the story is not just a dream, a fancy, or a metaphor. It is a *version* of things, perhaps no less true and yet no more final than other versions, an image thrown for a brief spell on the enchanted screen that the writer holds before us. As Penfield says (perhaps speaking for Doctorow himself): "It is the account in helpless linear translation of the unending love of our simultaneous but disynchrous lives" (291).

The critical reception of *Loon Lake* was on the whole positive, although nowhere near as enthusiastic as the response had been to *Ragtime*. Generally, the technical experiments with the novel's interior reality were found to be distracting. For example, Robert Towers wrote in *The New York Times Book Review* that "there were times when this reader felt trapped in a Barthian funhouse of mirrors and longed for some graspable, salient sense of the whole to emerge,"[7] and Clancy Sigal said in *New York* that "the style—some of it written in a kind of computer-printout blank verse, with side trips to Zen Japan—kept getting in the way."[8]

But most critics also found much to praise behind the technical fireworks. Thus, Towers commented on "the vivid human substance" of Doctorow's tale, and George Stade, reviewing the book for *The Nation*, called up the musical metaphor that the title for *Ragtime* had made inevitable when he praised *Loon Lake* as "odd and dissonantly beautiful, like a chorus of blues played by Dizzy Gillespie."[9] Stade felt this novel to be an advance on the politically doctrinaire *Ragtime* in its tone of gentle sympathy and ironic qualification as to Joe's struggle—the essential American struggle—to create one's self out of next to nothing. In *Loon Lake* "there is something still more valuable: a tone, a mood, an atmosphere, a texture, a poetry, a felt and meditated vision of how things go with us. It is more useful to a writer of fiction than a social conscience."

The novelist Margaret Atwood complimented the "many brilliant parts" of the novel and found it disappointing only in the hurried, arbitrary transformation of Joe Paterson into the Master of Loon Lake at the end.[10] Writing in *The Atlantic Monthly*, Benjamin DeMott claimed he liked some aspects of *Loon Lake* much better than he had some dimensions of *Ragtime:* "There are openings toward the human that give the book a freshness—a sweetness, even, that's absent from *Ragtime*."[11]

But the truth of a couple of critical dissents cannot be disregarded. In *The New Republic*, Mark Harris acknowledged the impressiveness of Doctorow's previous achievements but called this novel "a failed work of a serious man" and the production of "a writer halted in his work." He especially objected to the ending: "In the most indolent fashion Doctorow carries the life of Joe of Paterson 40 years forward with a two-page Who's Who entry concluding this novel. I cannot believe it. A high school creative writing class would never stand for such a thing."[12]

An even more vehement attack was that of Dean Flower in *The Hudson Review*, who loathed Doctorow's "suave new stylistic tricks," called the major effect of the novel "a sham," and argued that Doctorow had not created his characters and milieu out of original, deeply felt imagination but had instead sewn together his novel from literary scraps left over from Dos Passos, James T. Farrell, Steinbeck, and Richard Wright, "glazed over with a Mailer-style hipsterism." He claimed that Joe especially was a fake, a "mechanical pastiche of Gatsby, Willy Stark, and Rojack in Mailer's *An American Dream. . . .* Doctorow's figure remains stuffed, a set of fragments from other books."[13]

Having journeyed so far outward into self-delighting invention and cosmic paradox in the creation of *Loon Lake*, Doctorow will return to more traditional tones and narrative procedures for his next two books, *Lives of the Poets* and *World's Fair*.

Notes

1. Anthony Burgess, "Doctorow's Hit Is a Miss," *Saturday Review* Sept. 1980: 66.

2. Doctorow, *Loon Lake* (New York: Random House, 1980) 7. Further references will be noted parenthetically.

3. George Plimpton, ed., *The Writer's Chapbook* (New York: Viking, 1989): 69.

4. Carol C. Harter and James R. Thompson, *E. L. Doctorow* (Boston: Twayne, 1990) 128.

5. Richard Trenner, ed., *E. L. Doctorow: Essays and Conversations* (Princeton, N.J.: Ontario Review Press, 1983) 40.

6. Harter and Thompson 85.

7. Robert Towers, "A Brilliant World of Mirrors," *The New York Times Book Review* 28 Sept. 1980: 47.

8. Clancy Sigal, "The Howard Hughes Syndrome," *New York Magazine* 29 Sept. 1980: 49.

9. George Stade, "Types Defamiliarized," *The Nation* 27 Sept. 1980: 285–86.

10. Margaret Atwood, "E. L. Doctorow: Writing by His Own Rules," *Book World* 28 Sept. 1980: 1–2.

11. Benjamin DeMott, "Doctorow's Promise," *The Atlantic Monthly* (Sept. 1980): 107.

12. Mark Harris, "Books and the Arts: *Loon Lake*," *The New Republic* 20 Sept. 1980: 31, 32.

13. Dean Flower, "Fiction Chronicle," *Hudson Review* 34 Spring 1981: 105–06.

CHAPTER SIX

Lives of the Poets

The 1984 collection of six stories and a novella, *Lives of the Poets,* varies widely in quality as well as in the amount of autobiography Doctorow has put into the pieces. Two of the stories, "The Writer in the Family" and "Willi," are fluently written and cleverly plotted, and show in microcosm Doctorow's constant concerns. But two of the stories, "The Foreign Legation" and "The Leather Man," seem to be not quite successful experiments with voice and incident, and both have elements that seem forced and unconvincing, as if the material or the tone was not really compatible with Doctorow's sensibility. A very short piece called "The Water Works" (less than four pages) reads more like the opening paragraphs for a novel of fantasy-horror than a story complete in itself, but it is promising enough that one wishes that Doctorow would make another attempt to write in the genre he has to this point abandoned after *Big as Life.* And one of the stories, "The Hunter," is a small masterpiece.

Understanding E. L. Doctorow

"The Water Works" begins with a chase straight out of fiction by Edgar Rice Burroughs or Arthur Conan Doyle, or a film like *Blade Runner*: "I had followed my man here. Everything he did was mysterious to me, and his predilection for the Water Works this November day was no less so."[1]

Inside the echoing twilight within the Water Works there floats the corpse of an urchin "drowned blue," and, after the little body is recovered with slings and ropes by the city employees, "my man" makes off with the body at a suspiciously great speed in his carriage. Although the pursuer and his prey are not given any motivation or even identity in the thousand-word fragment Doctorow has chosen to publish here, the hints of some unholy Frankensteinian "resurrection" are pleasantly grisly, and "The Water Works," although amounting to little more than a sort of prose doodle, is a promising beginning for a tale of terror.

"Willi" is a story about the deathblow dealt to a family in a world that is trembling on the brink of extinction. Daniel Isaacson identified himself a "criminal of perception" when as a child he saw through the pretenses of the grown-up world into matters that a child was not supposed to comprehend. Willi becomes not only a criminal of perception but, caught in the toils of an overmastering experience, the agent of his family's destruction.

The story is told in retrospect several decades after its crucial events, a device Doctorow will use again in *Billy Bathgate*. The setting is Galicia, in central Europe, and the year is 1910. Willi, now a scientist of middle age, recalls that as a boy of thirteen—"the year a boy enjoys his initiation into manhood"—he was torn out of his harmony with things one idyllic summer's afternoon ("I was resonant with the hum of the universe" [33]) when he spies his mother in *flagrante delicto* in his father's barn with his own handsome young tutor, Ledig. Willi's reaction to the sight is a complex mixture of humiliation and eroticism, and Doctorow convinces the reader that this is just how a boy's mind *would* work with such an experience.

After the discovery, Willi is alienated from both his adored mother and the tutor who is his sole companion. As the son of a rich Jewish farmer, Willi is not allowed to mingle with the local peasant children, and his social isolation will magnify his hysteria. He feels "excommunicated" from his own life of thirteen years. And he will take revenge for that excommunication. With the primitive truth-weapon thrust into his hands by his "initiation," Willi will destroy his father's smooth, rational world and his mother's happy duplicity. Erotically excited into a wet dream by the memory of his mother in the act of betrayal, Willi goes to his father to exorcise the demon that seems to have made him "the archcriminal of my dreams" (41). His father is breeding hunting hounds, the female in heat restrained in a harness to ensure a safe and productive coupling with the

Understanding E. L. Doctorow

male: "Papa," Willi tells him, "they should be
named Mama and Ledig" (42). His words are devastating: "That night I heard from the bedroom
the shocking exciting sounds of her undoing" (44),
the middle-aged Willi recalls. And in an important
way his father's blows on his mother's body have
turned out to have anticipated the sound of beaten
flesh and the mix of pity and sexual excitement
that proto-Nazi hoodlums will create for Willi
when they punish street whores just after the
Great War, when the secure and reasonable world
of *Mitteleuropa* is lost indeed. This linkage between
microcosm and macrocosm, private experience
and historical event, is an imaginative connection
central to Doctorow's method.

"The Writer in the Family" is the most cleverly constructed of the tales in *Lives of the Poets*. Although more muted than "Willi," it is also a story
of family tension and family revenge. The premise
of the story is at once simple and yet promising:
the family's father, called only Jack, has died suddenly, and his own mother, ninety and mentally
disconnected from the world, is being kept from
the terrible knowledge that she's outlived her son.
Jack's sisters decide for the old woman's sake that
they will maintain the pretense that Jack can no
longer visit her in New York because he's moved to
Arizona for his bronchitis. Aunt Francis conde-
scendingly enlists the narrator, Jonathan, "the
writer in the family," to fake letters from his father,

as Jack would be presumed to write them from his new life in the Western desert.

Jonathan writes the letters and turns them over to his Aunt Frances for her to read to the near-senile grandmother, but his participation in the charade evolves into an imaginative involvement in his father's lifelong series of business failures and missed opportunities. In order to rectify with a writer's magic wand the cosmic injustice of Jack's mediocrity, Jonathan composes a final letter. In Jonathan's forgery "Jack" tells his mother that he has now sold his electrical appliance store "at a very fine profit" and reveals to his mother that he is *dying*—and not dying of the disease that claimed him in reality, but, as the writer in the family poeticizes it, "I am simply dying of the wrong life" (21). The reader grasps the essential insight: a son's deepened awareness of the gulf between the life his father lived and the life he *ought* to have lived. The clever stroke of using the false letter to tell a formidable truth gives the story its authority. And Doctorow has treated with sensitivity the jealousies and manipulations, the power struggles and desperate allegiances, that are forced upon us by the family, his abiding imaginative concern.

"The Foreign Legation" is set in an upscale suburb of New York City much like Doctorow's New Rochelle. The story begins with the disintegration of a family, for Morgan's wife has taken their children and left him, and it ends with a

literal big bang: Morgan is dazed and slightly injured in the bombing of one of the old-money
mansions that now houses a legation from some
unnamed Third World country whose political
turmoil conducts to terrorism. Times have
changed: this is the theme of the tale.

Although the reader never gets to know
enough about Morgan to sympathize with his
abandonment, Doctorow cleverly connects the
man's identity to the forces that move the world
culture. Morgan is the assistant curator of pre-
Columbian art at a specialized cultural museum in
New York City, and one senses that the disintegration of Morgan's marriage is in some small fashion
part of the world's drift toward a cultural transformation. His nightly jogging brings him into a microcosm of that cultural drift, and the imagery of
the story subtly enforces the likeness between the
disintegrative forces that blow apart Morgan's
marriage and the political violence that the West's
smug rationality cannot contain: "Homes were for
people's lives to explode in like those steel-mesh
hutches used by police bomb-disposal squads,"
Morgan muses (64), assuming like a good Yankee
that the reasonable assumptions of American civilization will continue to contain the danger and
frustrations that are obviously building up toward
flashpoint everywhere in a brave new world.

The last paragraphs of Doctorow's story are a
convincing evocation of what the experience of a
terrorist bombing must be like. In the profound

disorientation of the moments just after the explosion, Morgan's confusion of polite behavior with the responses appropriate to a catastrophe strikes the reader as exactly the right psychological touch: "He picked up, and put down again, a maroon knee sock with a child's leg in it" (75). And on seeing amidst the blood and twisted metal of the bombing's aftermath a woman jogger who'd once been rude to him, Morgan dazedly *apologizes* for his involvement in the explosion: "He was embarrassed. Did I do this? he said, trying to smile, trying to make himself presentable, smoothing his hair with his bloodied hand" (75).

"The Leather Man" is study in what might be called the official American police attitude. It is built around some sort of meeting among police detectives or theorists of political control in what seems to be Westchester County, and it reads like an excerpt from an electronic eavesdropping tape collected in a right-wing think tank. There is no action, only some political speculation from the police, whose normal quotient of paranoia has started to metastasize; collectively, they seem to fear the increasing possibility of a threat from the bottom elements of society to threaten society. And as with J. P. Morgan or Houdini or Evelyn Nesbit in *Ragtime*, the police speak with voices intellectually amplified by E. L. Doctorow.

The Leather Man of the title is evidently a hebephrenic or schizophrenic dysfunctional who roamed the Berkshires and Westchester County a century ago in a leather knight's costume of his own design, and one of the theorists uses him as an illustration that antisocial behavior in America has deeply rooted precedents. And as always with the political ultraright, things seem to them to be getting worse, for even if modern grotesques like the bag ladies and winos of the Lower East Side *seem* harmless, one must always be on guard: "What is new is the connection they're making with each other, some kind of spontaneous communication has flashed them into awareness of each other" (80).

Various examples of antisocial behavior are recounted by the reactionary theorists. There is an instance from the great hippie carnival of Woodstock, where the students and the acidheads and the draft dodgers and other crypto-revolutionary types gathered by the hundreds of thousands and perhaps hovered on the threshold of a sort of revolutionary critical mass, and the police watching over their behavior in the interests of law and order constituted "only one part per ten thousand, like the legal chemistry for a preservative" (81). There are examples from the destitute, homeless flotsam of the city, and from middle-class dropouts like the New Rochelle engineer who becomes one day a homeless Peeping Tom—peeping into his own home. The virus may strike anywhere. And the virus may become a plague. Even if the police cannot quite define the threat, *something* is in the air. As with most macho bull sessions, the discussion gets around to sex, and here Doctorow has his cops make a speculative leap, linking the psychic situation of the Leather Man to the ordinary varieties of American adultery: "It becomes your true life to . . . keep moving emotionally, you find finally the emotion in the movement. You are the Leather Man, totally estranged from society" (88).

Estrangement is also the substance of "The Hunter," a story of haunting and subtle beauty. It is winter in a dying factory town in upstate New York, and the nameless young woman who is the new schoolteacher "has been here just long enough for her immodest wish to transform these children to have turned to awe at what they are" (48). Doctorow gives his flower-child teacher just the sort of imagination, vitality, and narcissism that such a woman would possess. Instead of merely boring her children with spelling and long division, for example, she leads them all through the big, echoing, near-empty school building, telling them they are a "lost patrol in the caves of a planet far out in space." And, of course, in the deepest sense they *are*. And the teacher is not simply the cheery and sympathetic person who's not above doing somersaults along with the children on the gym mat, for Doctorow hints at a half-hidden, half-humiliating sexual frustration.

The schoolbus has a new driver, a blond young man, and the teacher finds herself interested in him; there is, after all, no one else in town. But there is a vexing social and intellectual gulf between them. The driver is just another underemployed, ignorant Joe and the teacher is put off almost against her will by the fact that he is common. The heart of her problem seems to be that the teacher is offended by the fact that the town is not even *trying* to make itself good enough for her. One of Doctorow's most effective touches is to have his teacher perform an act of smug noblesse oblige by reading aloud at the old people's home and then find herself shocked and repulsed by the vicious egotism of the senior citizens, who mock each other and fight for her attention.

If the schoolteacher is the hunter of the story's title, there is in the tale a literal hunter as well. Inspecting the myth-haunted ruins of the town's great mansion where the factory owner is said to have killed his bride in the house he built for her, the teacher sees from the second story a man with a rifle in an adjacent field; he fires a single shot into the mansion wall, then vanishes like a wraith.

Valium is her next attempt at putting her nerves in order, then a movie that only recalls her to her own isolation: "She sees her life exactly as it is outside the movie theater" (54). Then a trip to the local bar, where she meets the bus driver. Doctorow is an effective mimic, and the conversation between these mismatched human beings foreshadows the failure of their relationship even to begin:

What do you do to get to be a teacher?

You go to college. She sighs: What do you do to be a driver?

It's a county job, he says. You need a chauffeur's license and a clean record.

What is a dirty record?

Why, if you've been arrested, you know? If you have any kind of record. Or if you got a bad service discharge.

She waits.

I had a teacher once in the third grade, he says. I believe she was the most beautiful woman I have ever seen. I believe now she was no more'n a girl. Like you. But she was very proud and she had a way of tossing her head and walking that made me wish to be a better student. (56)

Although the teacher comes to admit to herself in the midst of this lame conversation that she really is intent on making her schoolchildren love her (Doctorow lightly brushes this need with sex, too), the bus driver's pass at her only enrages the teacher—at him, at herself, at her own sexual needs. The flower child suddenly becomes an outraged snob and denounces the driver as a "stupid goddamn mill hand" (58).

The story's last passage has a beauty difficult to paraphrase. Avoiding even the sight of the driver when the bus pulls in with the children Monday morning, the teacher announces that today is a special day, and the town photographer has been summoned to take a picture of the class. "I don't get these school calls till spring," the pot-bellied man in his string tie complains. "Why, these children ain't fixed up for their picture. . . . They ain't got on their ties and their new shoes. You got girls here wearing trousers" (59). But the picture is taken, the teacher holding as many of the children as she can get her arms around, her heart perhaps crying out in secret near-hysteria: *at least I have these!* In its delicacy and accuracy and grave, disciplined sympathy, "The Hunter" is an impressive achievement.

The title novella, "Lives of the Poets," is altogether different from the other pieces in the collection: funny, intimate, unstructured, garrulous, and seemingly autobiographical down to the fine details. If "The Writer in the Family" transforms elements of Doctorow's life into structured art held at arm's length, "Lives" seems to anticipate his 1985 novel-memoir, *World's Fair,* in its contagious fascination with that which was *only there.* We feel that almost everything here and in *World's Fair* is recovered rather than invented, and the play of intelligence upon reality is both the motive and the delight of the piece.

A man alone is in bad company, said Valéry. And it was W. H. Auden who quipped that Eros is the father of cities. Doctorow's persona, Jonathan, is not only alone in his new Greenwich Village writer's lair, but he is just turned fifty, and the dismal occasion of his birthday seems to have forced him into a discussion—if not quite an assessment—of his art and his life, his successes and his failures and his feelings. He has left his wife and children up in Connecticut and come down to New York, ostensibly to write. But Jonathan's wife has a host of suspicions about the real uses to which the apartment is being put, and the novella confirms the worst of them. Jonathan has a mistress: "I took it for her. I took it for our New York place" (168).

The title of the piece has been drawn from Samuel Johnson's *Lives of the Poets* (1779–81), but here Jonathan's "poets" are the writers and intellectuals, both men and women, who constitute the dramatis personae of his life: wife, lover, friends. Most of them seem to be "couples not entirely together" (104), and Jonathan's own marriage seems to be tottering. Even his success as a writer has something hollow in it: "Each book has taken me further and further out so that the occasion itself is extenuated, no more than a weak distant signal from the home station, and even that may be fading" (174-75).

And yet the tone of "Lives of the Poets" is not at all elegiac or despairing. Jonathan is in love, and the novella is a love letter. Just as with Warren Penfield and Joe Paterson "rediscovering" Clara from their pasts, Jonathan the writer was in love with his mistress long before he met her—or met her again. But the novella gives no indication how the affair will turn out, for although Jonathan proclaims that he has "the courage to give everything up for her," the woman seems content with a mere relationship and remains skeptical of Jonathan's resolve, suspecting he's more in love with the idea of being in love than in love with her. And the half-dozen marriages and love affairs that Jonathan finds crashing down around himself—the *loves* of the poets—are unequivocal disasters. So perhaps the affair will simply be allowed to stagger on toward an ultimate pratfall. "Lives" is not a carefully constructed love story like Philip Roth's *Goodbye, Columbus,* where human choices yield moral insight. It is a tale created out of that murkiest of mediums, the unsatisfactory stuff of real life. One of the least Jewish dimensions of an otherwise markedly Jewish persona in "Lives" is the absence of self-lacerating guilt in the clash between Eros and ethics. In this regard Doctorow's Jonathan seems only distantly related to Roth's Alex Portnoy, the most famous fictional self-flagellator of them all.

And yet Doctorow's novella is executed with a sensibility that can only be classified as late-twentieth-century American Jewish, an ironic mood that is as distinctive as it is difficult to define, and he will continue this mood on into his next book, *World's Fair.* Speaking of Jewish writers, Robert Alter holds that the distinctive atmosphere created by the Jewish imagination stems from the paradox of "an immense sadness of matter" sheathed in a "delightfulness of manner" in creating that peculiarly Jewish paradox, "the use of comedy as a last defense of the imagination against grim fate."[2] Philip Roth's career has demonstrated for us the formidable powers of a Jew's free-floating guiltiness, so when Jonathan informs us that it "may not be in my nature to be married" and that he loves a woman othe! than his wife, it is only right to expect a long, comic-mournful monologue concerning sexual-ethical shame. And there is indeed more than a touch of that in "Lives." For example, when Jonathan muses on the mailman's deliveries (one of the novella's devices is to give us a running account of the day's random-seeming, perception-provoking little events), he receives a postcard from his lover, mailed to him from Egypt. For a moment he is elated, but his Jewish guilt reflexes quickly kick in: "Happiness is intolerable for more than two seconds" (132).

And yet the Jewishness of "Lives" seems to spring more from matters political and humanitarian than from Jonathan's mid-life adulteries, and it is with that Manhattan sea wrack of immigrants that the "radical Jewish humanism" in Doctorow really gets itself expressed. Doctorow creates for Jonathan's five-thousand-year-old Jewish conscience the humane, mildly dangerous act which climaxes the piece and allows him to lift the guilt of his success. Brenda, an activist actress, sees Jonathan at a fund-raising talk given by a young American physician just back from a Latin American country. She takes him to an activist church on the Upper West Side, where he sees some wretched illegal aliens being cared for by the parish. Jonathan is last seen with a mestizo family living with him, complete with diapers, tortilla mix, and dried beans—and worries of how long they're actually going to stay here. But finally some sort of truce is worked out with his social conscience, for he has finally seemed to discover a way to atone for what America is doing down there in Latin America, "what I have to do to live with myself" (178). Jewish liberal guilt has seldom been so charmingly assuaged.

This lifting of guilt is important to Doctorow. His experimental play of 1978, *Drinks Before Dinner*, was a talky, static attempt to exorcise the demons of guilt and boredom which seem to dwell inside American success. In the play a man called only Edgar (Doctorow's first name) holds a gun on a distinguished and powerful dinner guest from Washington, Alan (a Nobel Laureate perhaps modeled on Henry Kissinger) at a New York dinner party. "What a charming and sympathetic man!" Edgar exclaims of Alan. "How dangerous. You hear behind his charming and sympathetic voice the computer clicks of missiles calculating their trajectory." Nothing comes of Edgar's menace to Alan—the gun is not even loaded—and the audience more or less has to agree with Alan's bitter denunciation of Edgar as one of "those hypocrites of privilege who condemns everything but relinquishes nothing, . . . one of those spiritual vandals who would like to be a revolutionary but hasn't the balls of a flea."

Reviewing *Lives of the Poets* in *The New Republic,* James Wolcott grumpily observed that "E. L. Doctorow is sneaking open the cupboard doors of his imagination and saying 'Welcome to the clutter.' "[3] Wolcott thoroughly disliked the collection, especially the title piece, which he found "an act of vanity"—and not obvious, proud, "imperial" vanity, either: "The vanity of *Lives of the Poets* . . . is crabbed and pettish, like the book itself. Doctorow is crawling into his drab little box of solitude to make himself look sensitive and unbought."

The collection was chosen by *The New York Times* as one of the ten best works for 1984, and Peter S. Prescott's glowing review in *Newsweek* was one of the best notices it received. "Better than any fiction I know, *Lives of the Poets* illuminates the sources from which fiction springs,"[4] Prescott proclaimed, and it was obvious that he was one of the few reviewers not put off by Jonathan's self-indulgent mid-life crisis. The obvious autobiographical content of the title novella absorbed almost all of the attention directed at the book, perhaps unfairly, for there are some interesting stories in it.

Notes

1. Doctorow, *Lives of the Poets* (New York: Avon, 1986) 25. Further references are to this edition and will be noted parenthetically.

2. Robert Alter, "Jewish Humor and the Domestication of Myth," *Veins of Humor*, ed. Harry Levin (Cambridge, MA: Harvard University Press, 1979) 163–64.

3. James Wolcott, "Rag Time," *The New Republic* 3 Dec. 1984: 31.

4. Peter S. Prescott, "The Creative Muse," *Newsweek* 19 Nov. 1984: 107.

CHAPTER SEVEN

World's Fair

$W_{orld's}$ *Fair* is sometimes read as an autobiography, but in certain significant ways the book should be considered above all as fiction. Doctorow has stated that it was his intention with *World's Fair* to "break down the distinction between formal fiction and the actual, palpable sense of life as it is lived."[1] Readers schooled on *The Book of Daniel*, *Ragtime*, and *Lives of the Poets* will already be aware that Doctorow's attitude toward facts is to regard them as mere facts, things that may or may not be as true as deeper, poetic truths; if a poetic truth needs to be substituted for those mere facts, then that substitution will unapologetically be made. "I have this concept of history as imagery, and therefore as a resource for writing," Doctorow told an interviewer on the publication of *World's Fair*.[2] Generally speaking, the details of the first-person book seem to have been little altered from "life as it is lived"—from life as Edgar Lawrence Doctorow and his family really lived it. But the structure of *World's Fair* is perhaps best understood as a design intended to generate the satisfactions of fiction, and, just as he did with the characters in *Ragtime*, the mature writer amplifies and reimagines the experiences of the child he once happened to be. And as a political writer he shapes even his autobiographical material toward a political argument, especially in regard to the naïve political assumptions that underlay the great World's Fair of 1939.

The fact that *World's Fair* is most centrally concerned with Doctorow's family relationships is of first importance in examining the book as an autobiography. "Neither in environment nor in heredity can I find the exact instrument that fashioned me, the anonymous roller that pressed upon my life a certain intricate watermark whose unique design becomes visible when the lamp of art is made to shine through life's foolscap,"[3] Vladimir Nabokov writes in his memoir, *Speak, Memory*. This is eloquently stated, but Doctorow, a great admirer of Nabokov's prose, might well disagree with two implications in Nabokov's metaphysics, and these points of disagreement help define his intentions and his interests. For Doctorow, his family would obviously be the "instrument" that, more than any other single force, "fashioned" him. He has written *World's Fair* to tell us how.

Perhaps an even more subtle point of disagreement, Doctorow might not subscribe to Nabokov's implication that art is so much more important than life. Indeed, Nabokov holds almost everywhere in his work that life itself is only a sort of styrofoam, intrinsically worthless, useful solely to protect art objects from suffering damage in transit from the point of their origin to the site of their display. No one believed more passionately in art for art's sake than the great Russian master; but Doctorow is in the final analysis a believer in art for *life's* sake. He is a moralist and a teacher. *World's Fair* is his tribute to family life, "life as it is lived," a family memoir more than a private memoir, and one created with neither propaganda nor sentimentality nor condescension. The fictional techniques he will apply to this account of his life and the life of his family are meant to enhance its meaning, not replace it with another kind of meaning altogether.

Literary autobiography offers three primary sorts of fascination. First, there is the play of memory on reality, for few human acts are so pleasant to experience vicariously as the act of recall, no matter what the object, no matter how trivial the detail. Secondly, there is the satisfaction of discovering the "original" of things found in the mature fiction. *World's Fair* has several of these prenatal shadow forms, some of them important in comprehending Doctorow's stories and novels. And thirdly, there is that delight peculiar to all biography and autobiography: the prophetic awareness that an ordinary childhood leads toward the extraordinary maturity about which the reader already knows. No other narrative mode has a comparable power of spinning life's straw into gold. *World's Fair* is thus, along with much else, a prophecy, and a prophecy magically fulfilled. The reader takes as much satisfaction in watching things come out as he knows they will as in finding out how destiny turned the trick in the first place.

One passage in the book is especially striking in regard to the third and simplest of these three effects. The Ringling Brothers and Barnum & Bailey Circus has come to Madison Square Garden; Doctorow, at seven or eight, thrills to the spectacle. But the spectacle includes one gag that Doctorow will use as a metaphor for his own future success. A wistful clown climbs the high wire and flounders about hilariously, seeming to risk his neck with his clumsiness and scaring the audience half to death. Of course that same clown proves to be the star aerialist. "I took profound instruction from this hoary circus routine,"[4] Doctorow declares. He makes the equation, even as a child: the clumsy clown is a disguised star; so, too, his own childhood—"the comic being of a little kid"—is merely an ugly duckling phase. Doctorow in the circus audience is outwardly a "sniffler with a red nose," but he knows that he will "someday in my good time reveal myself to be a superman among men" (147).

And so, of course, he has. The reader is always aware of Doctorow's future success assembling itself from the debris of what Nabokov called

"life's foolscap." *World's Fair* conveys to us between the lines a sense that the future knew all
along what it was up to, tinkering around here in
the past. Perhaps Edgar Doctorow at that young
age did not really know that he would turn out to
be a highly regarded, highly rewarded artist in
later life, "a superman among men," but that very
artist in his maturity is searching back through the
random-seeming materials of life for a means of
expressing destiny's design; the artistic point is
validated by the real event.

As for the more complex matter of biographical realities that Doctorow has used in his books,
one can see that a great many of his most remarkable fictional effects are grounded in his personal
history and that he has been able to achieve some
of his best things by a process more akin to imita-
tive fusion than strict invention. For example, *The
Book of Daniel* is a stronger book than was *Welcome
to Hard Times* or *Loon Lake* to the degree that Doctorow was able to graft his imagined Isaacson family onto his own real experience. Thus, Paul and
Rochelle are obviously taken from parents found
in *World's Fair.* Like Doctorow's father, Paul strikes
one less as a committed revolutionary than an
amiable idler from the CCNY cafeteria whose radical chic braggadocio conducts, step by astonishing
step, to his electrocution. And the Rochelle of *The
Book of Daniel* is seemingly modeled on the Rose
Altschuler Doctorow has given us in *World's Fair*—
less a Joan of Arc following celestial voices to the

fires of her martyrdom than a passionate avenger of the petit bourgeois poverty American capitalism has made her fate.

This transference from life into fiction seems to have occurred not only in terms of character study but also in less obvious ways. Just as one small example of a procedure that occurs scores of times, the giant aliens in *Big as Life* might have been suggested to the mature artist by the childhood sight of the mighty *Hindenburg* ("She was tilted toward me as if she were an enormous animal leaping from the sky in monumental slow motion. . . . The enormity of her was out of scale with everything" [198]) that astonished Doctorow on 6 May 1937, as it swam above the Bronx on the way to its spectacular death at Lakehurst, New Jersey. But then those giants might have been suggested by a more obvious source, for the 1939 World's Fair itself displayed "an enormous man made of Plexiglass . . . with all his giant internal organs visible, but no visible penis . . ." (327). Also, in our more humane era it comes as a shock to discover that the World's Fair had its freak shows, too, and it would be hard not to connect the pathetic creatures in Sim Hearn's carny in *Loon Lake* to their real counterparts at World of Tomorrow's "Odditorium" that Doctorow saw in 1939.

Red Bloom's gift for jazz in *Big as Life* may well have been created out of Doctorow's older brother Donald's fascination with the music, and Donald, Rose Doctorow, and the wealthy Aunt Frances who played a crucial role in "The Writer in the Family" are actually invited into the text of *World's Fair* to give us their observations and contribute to the prose time capsule that is Doctorow's project here. The narrative is thus given the quality of a sort of folk artifact, a chorus of family voices and imaginations. Doctorow called the book a novel, but it is certainly not the sort of fiction that Doctorow had previously published.

But the pleasures of *World's Fair* are by no means confined to connecting the numbered dots that link fiction to life. Mark Twain called *Huckleberry Finn* "a hymn to boyhood," and Wordsworth (lines from *The Prelude* form the epigraph to *World's Fair*) subtitled his poem "The Growth of a Poet's Mind." Either or both of those descriptive tags would fit Doctorow's autobiography just as well. He is a tender, patient archaeologist and an extraordinary musician.

There is school, where the narrator is a good "citizen" and a good student. There are the movies, of course, and there is that archetypal American-boy discovery, baseball. The narrator (and it is surely significant that Doctorow uses his own first name, Edgar) loses the family dog to his own allergies and his father's duplicity, and we keenly feel the loss for ourselves. A brilliantly described Rockaway Beach in 1936 is not only rendered with intensity, but Doctorow also convinces the reader that the scene really did convey to him a primal sense of nothing less than the world itself: "I learned the enlightening fear of the planet" (79). 1936 was a good year for learning about fear, enlightening or otherwise, for in Europe "Jewish death was spreading" (127), and Doctorow conveys just the way in which a child's mind draws the world's evils in shapes comprehensible to its own size and place; real anti-Semitism finds him out in the form of some tough Irish bullies. His harrowing description of their menace brings hatred before the reader as journalism can never do.

Just as in *The Book of Daniel* and *Ragtime*, the accuracy and precision of a microcosm become one's means of apprehending the energies that are blazing across the surface of history. At the 1939–40 World's Fair a time capsule sponsored by Westinghouse was buried for the edification of the people of five thousand years from now, its contents such insignia of our civilization as *Gone with the Wind*, a Mickey Mouse plastic cup, a film of Howard Hughes flying around the world, and the Lord's Prayer in no fewer than three hundred languages. Scores of other children no doubt imitated that time capsule just as Doctorow did when he buried his Tom Mix Decoder badge, M. Hohner Marine Band harmonica, and four-page biography of Franklin Delano Roosevelt (with its grade of 100) in a foil-lined mailing tube. But of course the *real* time capsule he has given the future is the memoir itself. Time, said Auden, loves words and forgives all those who live by them, and this memoir is a perfect illustration of the truth of the poet's claim.

There is here the lost world of the radio drama, as charmingly recaptured as in Woody Allen's *Radio Days*. Here the reader finds *Ventriloquism Self-Taught*, a Haldeman-Julius Little Blue Book No. 1278; almost every American boy born before 1950 must have tried to teach himself ventriloquism, hypnotism, or "self-defense" from a badly printed pamphlet arriving in the mail. There are sword fights with wooden slats, ball games peculiar to the hard surfaces of a city, an account of a contest at the Polo Grounds between the Giants and the Dodgers *football* teams. The sudden rivalry-flirtation between boys and girls on the American schoolyard is done with a tender accuracy, for it is at school that the young Edgar begins to discover the astonishing fact of gender: "You found weaknesses and went chasing after them, like the cheetah, which I knew was, for short distances, the fastest animal in the world. The weakness of girls was their underpants" (139).

Sex is also and inevitably one of the crucial concerns of most memoirs, and although this memoir ends just after the narrator turns nine years old (and it is a narrative that recounts nothing that even begins to be lurid or embarrassingly "tough"), sex is a significant force in *World's Fair*. It is the invisible enemy that isolates young Edgar from his parents:

I secretly grieved for the dark mysterious things
my parents did in the privacy of their relationship. I didn't know quite what these things were,
but I knew they were shameful, requiring darkness. . . . This aspect of my parents' life lay like a
shadow on my mind. My mother and father, rul-
ers of the universe, were taken by something over
which they had no control. . . . The devastating
truth was that there were times when my parents
were not my parents; and I was not on their
minds. (98–99)

It is with his friend Meg and her mother that
Edgar discovers an even more intimate ache and
isolation as he finds the world larger and stranger
and more dangerous than the safe circle of his own
family. Playing with Meg he finds himself in his
first vaguely sexual games, and, finally invited to
the World's Fair, he watches Meg's pretty mother,
Norma, the fiancée of a cabdriver, swimming the
part of a mermaid and getting herself undressed
in a underwater strip show called "Oscar the Amorous Octopus."

Without embarrassment or condescension
Doctorow re-creates the properties of a real mind
and an authentic personality, alive in a particular
place: his memoir is part Nabokov, part Philip
Roth, part Norman Rockwell, and it conducts to a
skillfully achieved ending. Doctorow uses the
World's Fair of 1939–40 to climax his memoir. Here
he plays the role of novelist rather than that of auto-
biographer, for the symmetry of this set piece allows the book to end with an ironic effect rather

than mere reported event. Yet in spite of the arti-
ficiality of the passage, using the Fair to finish the
memoir is an intriguing device, for the naïveté and
preposterousness and optimism of the World of
Tomorrow causes the reader to see that the 1930s
were to be the last decade when it was still possible to believe that science would see to it that the
world's future would be happier than its past.
And it would obviously be the last time in his life
when Doctorow could see the Muse of History as a
benign prophetess of progress and light, uplift and
reason. Thus, he uses images for political-moral
effect just as he does in earlier works.

Edgar visits the Fair twice, and the two visits
are differentiated from each other in order to point
up the boy's growing powers of awareness—and
the darkening world beyond the Bronx, trembling
on the brink of war, that increasingly impinges on
his consciousness. If one agrees with Richard Eder
of the *Los Angeles Times* that "Doctorow evokes
Edgar's maturing with something close to magic,"
then a good place to find that magic is in these de-
scriptions of the Fair, for it is Eder's sound observation that while "there is nothing remarkable
about this or about any of the events and memo-
ries of Edgar's childhood," it is strictly the fine
"quality of recollection and narration"[5] that gives
the account its power.

Strangely, R. Z. Sheppard complained in *Time*
that "*World's Fair* is not a happy book. The drear-
iness of the '30s and the strains of family life

appear to have had a bad effect on Edgar's style. He is either too terse or verbosely academic, as if the boy grew up to be a literary critic rather than a novelist."[6] Although there is no way to finally "prove" anything one way or the other in disagreements over matters of literary tone, this seems a startling sort of judgment to make after reading passages of such frank, unequivocal happiness evoked in Edgar's heart by the great Fair. For example, finally seeing the Trylon and Perisphere, Edgar finds himself "incredibly happy. I felt like jumping up and down, I felt myself trembling with joy" (321).

The first visit is a marvelous success. Everything is "dazzling": the miniaturized Futurama "was a toy that any child in the world would want to own" (325), Frank Buck's Jungleland better than one had dared hope, the Siamese twins really were joined at the hip, the eight-foot English giant who sold the children a dimestore ring "seemed a kind man, if bored by what he was doing" (339). And even if going off the parachute jump with Meg terrifies Edgar, the ride allows him to prove his courage to her. He loves Meg and he loves her carefree, unabashed mother, whom he's now seen as a naked mermaid wrestling a rubber octopus. Life is more various and thrilling than he had known it could be, and if he just remembers to give himself without hesitation to this mysterious, fascinating world outside the circle of his protective family, perhaps he can survive to enjoy it.

Doctorow conveys this insight with dignity and precision: "I had worried before, all the time in this enormous effort to catch up to life, to find it, to feel it, comprehend it; but all I had to do was be in it and it would instruct me and give me everything I needed" (348).

The second trip to the Fair is arranged with a novelist's eye for contrast to the first. The tone and the placement of the scene at this climactic position in the book seems designed to create a different and purposefully ironic effect. The reader is intended to realize that the ordered, reasonable, forward-looking World of Tomorrow, with its Trylons and Perispheres and charming national pavilions serving national delicacies, is in actuality hurrying toward the shadow of Hitler, the Holocaust, and the Bomb—toward the catastrophe that Doctorow is indicating is its appointment with fate.

Even more ironically, Edgar wins the second trip to the Fair by gaining honorable mention in a citywide essay contest on the "typical American boy." He is a fine example of American youth—a letter from the Fair's governor, Grover Whalen, attests to this—and he can take his whole family for a free day at the exposition. This is a wonderful stroke of luck because a trip out to Flushing Meadow is an expense his family can ill afford, now that his father has lost the family musical instrument business in the Depression. As for the essay, given to us verbatim in all its awkward and endearing hopefulness ("The typical American boy is not fearful of Dangers. He should be able to go out in the country and drink raw milk. . . . He knows the value of a dollar. He looks death in the face" [35]), R. Z. Sheppard observes that Doctorow's "fawning entry" is heavy with irony for those who know his career, for "it introduces a writer who knows what it takes to get on the bestseller list."[7]

This second trip to the Fair confers a sort of heroism on Edgar, now the host for his own family, and the Trylon and Perisphere "granted some sort of beneficence to my shoulders" (361). But he is now also forced to see the great exhibition through the skeptical eyes of his father, and the wonderful Fair has deteriorated as the crowds have thinned. The shadow of history has fallen across the papier-mâché kingdom of illusions. Even a boy Edgar's age knows that the headlines bring only evil news these days. Poland has been invaded, rabbis are washing the cobblestones of Nuremberg, Japan has conquered China, another great and terrible war is perhaps only a heartbeat away. This second trip to the Fair is underlit with a new sense of isolation and vulnerability; far from being the image of the perfected form of what the world will one day surely come to be, the Fair is now the emblem of a naïve, impossible aspiration.

Seeing the "Immortal Well" of concrete and steel, site of the buried Time Capsule waiting to

inform the earthlings of 6939 about a vanished culture dead for five millennia, Edgar's father speaks
with disdain of the greedy, pretending civilization he sees all about him: this world of 1940, he
tells his family, will seem small and grotesque and
primitive to the enlightened people of five thousand years from now, for our world will be defined
by the fact that we spoke in an irreconcilable
"babble of tongues," and that we "murdered each
other and read abominable books." He rhetorically
quizzes his sons as to why the capsule contains
Gone with the Wind but "no hint from the stuff they
included that America has a serious intellectual
life, or Indians on reservations or Negroes who
suffer from race prejudice" (365). Doctorow is too
craftsmanlike to editorialize here on the failed ide-
alism of the Fair, but the last glimpses we have of
it are of Edgar's mother drifting toward the Jewish
Palestine pavilion ("They show that Jews can be
like everyone else") and his father making an
ironic condolence call to the Czechoslovakian pavilion because "Chamberlain betrayed them to
Hitler" (367). The father is sorry that the Soviet pavilion is gone and he cannot pay tribute to that noble experiment in social transformation, but Edgar
is even sorrier to discover that Meg's mother and
Oscar the Amorous Octopus have vanished too,
replaced by some routine sideshow acts and a
Dodgem bumper-car ride. And finally, the day he
has won for his family over and night falling, the

World's Fair itself is reduced to fireworks going up and "lighting the rain as if some battle were being fought between the earth and the sky" (368).

Reviewing *World's Fair* for *The New York Times*, Christopher Lehmann-Haupt indicated that the power of the book lay in its ability to do fine things with very ordinary materials: "you shake your head in disbelief and ask yourself how he has managed to do it. . . . You get lost in *World's Fair* as if it were an exotic adventure. You devour it with the avidity usually provoked by a suspense thriller. . . . [The vanished particulars of the 1930s] are savored in retrospect by a mature intelligence whose memory of childhood is so uncannily vivid, yet who keeps his unsentimental distance with the mock solemn prose that has become Mr. Doctorow's inimitable music."[8] And even though another *New York Times* reviewer, David Leavitt, found the book sometimes not to his liking because of what he called its "fractured and inconsistent feel," Leavitt praised Doctorow's gift for producing "magnificent descriptive passages."[9] Richard Eder and other reviewers pointed out the legacy owed by Doctorow to James Joyce's *Portrait of the Artist as a Young Man*: "His Daedalus lacks wings, but manages perfectly well on the subway," Eder said, and spoke of the prose of the book with great admiration. Bruce Weber noted the Joyce connection by commenting that Doctorow "uses the Bronx much as Joyce used Dublin—as a window on society."[10] But the difference between the intentions of the two writers is revealing, for Joyce was not content with the Dublin he found before him and spent the last thirty years of his career transforming the city into the mythical, surreal kingdoms of *Ulysses* and *Finnegans Wake*. Doctorow's intention was to recover the emotions and artifacts peculiar to the first decade of his life, deriving from those things only that which was really in them. It is the difference between artificer and archaeologist.

Notes

1. Bruce Weber, "The Myth Maker: The Creative Mind of Novelist E. L. Doctorow," *New York Times Magazine* 21 Oct. 1985: 78.

2. Weber 80.

3. Valadimir Nabokov, *Speak, Memory*, rev. ed. (New York: Putnam, 1966) 25.

4. Doctorow, *World's Fair* (New York: Fawcett, 1985) 146–47. Further references will be noted parenthetically.

5. Richard Eder, "World's Fair," *Los Angeles Times* 24 Nov. 1985: 3.

6. R. Z. Sheppard, "The Artist as a Very Young Critic," *Time* (18 Nov. 1985): 3.

7. Sheppard 107.

8. Christopher Lehmann-Haupt, "World's Fair," *The New York Times* 24 Nov. 1985: 12.

9. David Leavitt, "Looking Back on the World of Tomorrow," *New York Times Book Review* 10 Nov. 1985: 3, 25.

10. Weber 25.

CHAPTER EIGHT

Billy Bathgate

"The Americans are certainly great hero worshippers, and always take their heroes from the criminal classes," wrote Oscar Wilde from St. Joseph, Missouri, in 1882, in the midst of the New World tour that would seal his fame. "Outside my window about a quarter mile to the west stands a little yellow house and a crowd of people are pulling it down. It is the house of the great train robber and murderer, Jesse James, who was shot by his pal last week, and the people are relic hunters. . . . His doorknocker is to be offered for sale this afternoon, the reserve price being about the income of an English bishop."[1]

Billy Bathgate is a novel about the criminal classes. Its animating energy is indeed a species of hero worship, and the "disreputable genre materials" Doctorow says he likes to start from may well have derived from the comic book and the Depression-era pulp thriller. Doctorow seems to have tried to give his novel the joyful velocity and preposterousness of what the literary establishment would call "subliterature." *Billy Bathgate* is an attempt to elevate crime-thriller subliterature into art, just as *Lolita: Or the Confessions of a White Widowed Male* is an attempt to raise pornography to art. To try to make its origins respectable is to miss the point. Some of America's best novelists admit that they never got over the Great Bad Books, the Hollywood B-movies, the three-color Sunday funnies.

Doctorow has declared that "a novelist is a person who lives in other people's skins," and for his eighth novel he has gotten inside the skin of a fatherless Bronx kid who calls himself Billy Bathgate and happens to fall in with one of the Depression's most ruthless and fascinating gangsters, Arthur Flegenheimer, known as Dutch Schultz. The novel begins with Billy's presence at a gangland killing out in the midnight waters of New York Harbor, a scene spellbinding and preposterous in about equal measure. It is a comic-book opening, a pulp-thriller opening, the best moment in the novel. Recall that when Doctorow described finding the narrative formula that would allow him to go forward with *The Book of Daniel*, he spoke of his discovery of a tone and method that were "reckless" and "irresponsible"; in *Billy Bathgate* we sense the same sort of abandon.

"Nobody said not to so I jumped aboard and stood at the rail,"[2] Billy, a fifteen-year-old lackey for the gang, tells the reader many years after the event. As usual, Doctorow has taken pains to amplify a naïve intelligence with his own, and Billy does not speak to the reader as an uneducated fifteen-year-old, but as a mature and cultivated sensibility recalling the experiences of his youth. And so the Billy of middle years goes on to recount the killing of Dutch's henchman Bo Weinberg, a classic crime rub-out right down to the tub of cement around the man's feet, with the crime czar coldly making the murdered man's girlfriend watch. It is a scene that is not actually completed until much later in the book, when the last grisly details of Bo's destruction are recounted in what Peter S. Prescott of *Newsweek* calls "all its marvelous, hair-raising detail."[3] Doctorow has saved the particulars for a second climax. Bo's cement overshoes quickly harden, and the little tub in which he is standing imprisoned is fitted out with a rubber-wheeled dolly to roll the gangster over the side. But of course he is made to wait for his own death, tormented by his humiliation as well as his fear, and the Billy of 1935 abetted by the Billy of 1989 is there to record every nuance:

> Later he whispers to me take care of my girl don't let him do it to her get her away before he does her too, do I have your promise? I promise, I tell him in the first act of mercy in my life. . . . [But soon] Mr. Schultz in his shirtsleeves and suspenders appeared and came up behind him and lifted one stockinged foot and shoved it in

the small of Bo's back, and the hands broken
from their grasp and the body's longing lunge for
balance where there was none, careening leaning
backward he went over into the sea and the last
thing I saw were the arms which had gone up,
and the shot white cuffs and the pale hands reaching for heaven. (160, 162)

As in *Loon Lake*, a Horatio Alger miracle allows Billy the underage nobody to get himself ini-
tiated into the most dangerous, glamorous gang in
New York. Dutch sees Billy juggling near one of
his Bronx illegal beer barns and is charmed
enough by the lad's discipline and cool to take him
on as an amusement and an apprentice. Millionaire adopts guttersnipe, just as Dan Cody takes in
Jay Gatsby.

Billy is led by degrees into the inner sanctum
of the Schultz gang, with its "purveyed lawless
might and military self-sufficiency . . . so thrilling
to boys" (24), a lad useful to Dutch and his men
because, like any captain of industry, the gangster
needs eyes and ears and a face the police don't
know to run errands, to tail people, to report back:
a spy. Thus the novel has its privileged narrator,
privy to secrets but distanced enough for his voice
to lend a moral and intellectual dimension to the
raw action. The United States is the country of the
creation of the self, and the crime novel is one
of the truest variants of the American national *Bildungsroman*. From *The Great Gatsby* to William

Kennedy's *Legs*, the romance of high crime has en-
gaged some of America's best writers. There is the
sheer escapism of the thing. As Billy puts it, he
risks his life to join the Dutch Schultz gang and
live in a "thrilling state of three-dimensional danger" (39). Doctorow has written his novel so the
reader can do the same.

New York, 1935. As with *Loon Lake*, the novel
of Doctorow's which it most closely resembles,
Billy Bathgate is set in the era of Doctorow's own
childhood, and to its atmosphere he has devoted
many pages of his best descriptive prose. Stephen
Schiff remarked in *Vanity Fair* that Doctorow is "a
masterly stylist of the Lush, Gorgeous Prose
school (no Raymond Carver minimalism here,
thank you)."[4] Certainly it is a vivid, precise,
anachronistic New York, like a stereopticon slide.
Apples are five cents each, and since October 1929
you might even get to buy one from a former
Wall Street stockbroker. Peaches on the Bronx's
Bathgate Avenue, "this bazaar of life," are eight
cents a pound. There are breadlines, hobos,
Hoovervilles. What we call "soul music" is known
as "race music" in 1935, and Tammany Hall is the
name for a vast spiderwork of favors and patron-
age and bribery just beneath the surface of New
York political life. A boy can save carfare by cling-
ing to the backside of an electric trolley, and the
basketball sneakers that help him hold on might
well be autographed by Nat Holman, just as Billy's

are. It has been said that God lives in details, and Doctorow has provided them in delicious prodigality. As for his plot, it is pure and defiant daydream, as essentially unreal as a James Bond novel. After the cautious and appealing fidelity to life of *World's Fair*, Doctorow has gone to the other extreme, and his crime novel bears only the sketchiest relationship to observed reality. In consequence, the reader never really believes in Billy or Dutch or the others, and we never for a moment fear *for* them. This is a heavy price for a writer to pay for creating daydream thrills.

Perhaps sensing this deficiency, Doctorow has attempted to heighten his prose, and instead of the understated precision that marked *Ragtime* and *World's Fair*, *Billy Bathgate* is written with a sort of Faulknerian excess, with some of its sentences running half a page and the vocabulary charged with overkill. The book is never boring, but we are never *involved* in it in as we are with Doctorow's best work. As George Orwell said of the characters in some of Dickens's novels, ''They start off as magic-lantern slides and they end by getting mixed up in a third-rate movie.''[5]

Bo Weinberg dead, the girl Drew Preston becomes Dutch's prize, and Billy is assigned to watch her. He accompanies her back to her sumptuous Manhattan apartment, the likes of which he has seen before only on the silver screen and the sophistication of which allows Doctorow the same sort of ironic leverage for comic description that Twain derived from Huck Finn gawking at the Grangerford decor. For example, urns in the foyer are decorated with "Greek philosophers holding wrapped sheets around themselves" (42). Even more Greek is the spectacle of Drew's husband, Harvey, in an embrace with a nameless young male, but the men are hardly disconcerted. When Harvey languidly asks his wife what became of Bo Weinberg ("you were so gaga about him"), her reply is a classic instance of aristocratic understatement: "Well if you must know, he died" (43). Doctorow manufactures this sort of fun from the social gulf between the cafe-society world from which Drew Preston springs and the guttersnipe world of the East Bronx, which is in many instances a grotesque parody of its upper-class analogue. When he is not being melodramatic, Doctorow generates some familiar but amusing social satire.

Dutch's gang is composed of underworld denizens as colorful as the cast of a comic book. There is a hood called Lulu Rosenkrantz of the garlic breath and Mickey the driver who says nothing ("his intelligence was all in his meaty hands" [73]) and the faithful foot soldier Irving who does whatever he is told. Most successful of all in the supporting cast is Otto "Abbadabba" Berman, the dapper, hunchbacked mathematical genius who serves as the brains of the gang, a "deviously instructive" presence of perfect reserve and solemn wisdom. Since Billy is fatherless and his laundress mother is as disconnected from reality as Daniel Isaacson's grandmother, the gang becomes his new family. Once again Doctorow's fascination with the family asserts itself.

Strange family. Billy watches Dutch kill a greedy fire inspector with his bare hands and stuff his corpse into a garbage can. Troublesome window washers trying to establish their own union are allowed to fall to their deaths from scaffolding fif teen stories high right before Billy's eyes. Dutch tells Billy about cutting the throat of a rival numbers- racket boss in a barbershop, a piece of clever professional work with chloroform and razorblade of which the crime boss is extremely proud and a passage on which Doctorow has lavished his most craftsmanlike attention. Billy's gift for juggling a few stray objects in the air has led the boy into a dark, thrilling realm just behind the façade of the reasonable world, and he will never submit to the commonplace existence again. "Life held no grandeur for a simple thief" (271). Billy's "enlistment" is not only an education; it is an identity.

The scene shifts to upstate New York, just as it did in *Loon Lake*, where Dutch is preparing the jury for his upcoming trial for tax evasion by injecting large doses of cash into the local economy. This is the first pastoral scene Billy has ever encountered, so very different from the teeming, dirty avenues of the slums, "where the natural world was visible only in globules of horse manure pressed flat by passing tires" (215). Billy learns the magic that lives in guns when he learns to shoot, watches a disloyal union boss assassinated, and hears Dutch cheerfully reminisce about blinding a rival. Daydreams being daydreams, he even gets to sleep with Drew Preston while he is supposedly chaperoning her at the Saratoga racetrack, a far cry from the two-for-a-dollar rooftop sex he has experienced back in the East Bronx with his small "witchy" orphan friend, Rebecca.

But Dutch's career and life are on the down curve. Billy had juggled "in adoration of our great gangster of the Bronx," but now *Götterdämerung* is at hand. "He had risen and he was falling" (281). Special prosecutor Thomas E. Dewey is closing in on Dutch's tax predicament, and when Dutch discovers that even his bribery money has turned unacceptable in the city, he retreats to New Jersey to perfect a scheme for assassinating Dewey. This is a mortal mistake. Other gang bosses want anything but an open assassination, for even Depression-era America is not quite lost to the cynicism of a banana republic just yet, and these bosses protect the destruction of their system with an assassination of their own. Dutch's gang is attacked at the Palace Chophouse in Newark on 23 October 1935, and of course Billy is there to tell the reader about it, standing hidden on a toilet seat while Dutch is desperately wounded with .45 slugs while still trying to button his fly. The novel is a daydream, and Billy's invisibility is a daydream state.

Lulu and Irving are dead, and Berman the mathematician has only breath to whisper in Billy's ear a few last numbers—the combination to Dutch's portable safe, the contents of which prove to be $362,112, surely enough for Billy and his mother to purchase new lives. But Doctorow is still not done with his prose daydream. "Murders are exciting and lift people into a heart-beating awe as religion is supposed to do" (305), Billy observes. And Dutch is still tenuously alive. There are still fabulous secrets.

Billy not only attends to Dutch's last hours in the Newark hospital, he even eats the crime czar's last meal for him (consommé, roast pork, lime Jell-O). Then, now invisible behind a folding partition of cotton cloth (but really behind an author's indifference to even the sketchiest sort of likelihood), Billy takes down the man's last soliloquy with a pencil stub he keeps sharpening with his thumbnail. "He died dispensing himself in utterance . . . as if all we are made of is words and when we die the soul of speech decants itself into the universe" (308).

Dutch's words contain cryptic information that only Billy can decode, for the police reporters on the other side of the partition hoping to capture some clue to the whereabouts of Dutch's hidden loot are confounded by his hallucinatory monologue. But Billy grasps the hidden meaning of one of the dying gangster's sentences: "Money is paper too and you stash it in the shithouse" (310),

and he and his orphan pal Arnold Garbage recover an immense fortune in an unbunged beer
barrel from the "shit and refuse" on the floor of
one of Dutch's old beer barns. Doctorow's cornu-
copia of miracles is still not exhausted: "From that
midnight we became partners in a corporate enter-
prise that goes on to this very day" (319), Billy tells
us enigmatically. And magically, Billy's mother re-
gains most of her mental balance, and soon Billy
goes back to high school, and then on to "an Ivy
League college I would be wise not to name," then
to a lieutenant's commission in the army and certain hush-hush work in World War II, returning
magically unharmed, and he magically unearths
somewhere yet *more* of Dutch's "pirate swag," millions and millions of dollars of it "stuffed in a safe,
packed in mail sacks" (321). And just as in *Loon
Lake*, Doctorow *still* has a final magic twist of plot
up his sleeve.

Even though the murder of Dutch and Berman have made Billy "feel fatherless again, a
whole new wave of fatherlessness" (303), the
novel ends with a restoration of the circle of family
even more stunningly unforeseen than Bennett's
adoption of Joe at the conclusion of *Loon Lake*. Billy
does not find another father, he becomes one. A
liveried chauffeur delivers to the new apartment
he shares with his mother nothing less than the
son he has sired with Drew Preston, and, like
Mother in *Ragtime*, Billy's mother receives the
child serenely, as if she realizes intuitively she has

been selected, blessed. "My life as a boy was over," Billy declares (322), and the three of them will live, the reader can be sure, happily ever after, Billy's apprenticeship with evil now redeemed.

Stephen Schiff is correct in his assessment of Doctorow's use of popular culture and disreputable genre materials as the point of departure for his stories and novels:

> When you trace the fantasy materials that recur throughout his fiction, they look almost touchingly boyish and antiquated: gangsters and cowpokes; broken-spirited poets; tough but frail-looking blondes whisked out of reach by sleekly dangerous hooligans. If Doctorow is indeed the artist as conduit, then what he's channeling is the great American dreamwork: his materials are the stuff of our legends—and our schlock.[6]

Perhaps especially in *Billy Bathgate* the reader is constantly aware of Doctorow's use of junk from the pulp and celluloid bins of 1930s mass art. But just as he was able in *Ragtime* to fill in the outlines of historical personages with a vivid life of his own invention and to reclaim overfamiliar situations from the attic of American popular culture, so here in his big crime novel the force of his intelligence transforms the preposterous characters and plots from the comic-strip kingdom of schlock into a creation that rewards our mature attention. Doctorow spoke in an interview of purposely choosing to go back to the mind of a young boy in order to lend once more a sense of wonder and what he called "empowerment" to the voice of his narration, "a kind of rhapsodic appreciation of what adults have stopped thinking about."[7] Boys' adventures, he has noted, were the genesis for memorable tales from such masters of boys' fiction as Twain, Dickens, and Robert Louis Stevenson.

"At his best," says Schiff, "Doctorow is able to reimagine [these humble materials] from the ground up, and to reignite the moral and political issues buried in their ashes. Doctorow is like a medium for our dead fictions; as they flow through him, they come out alive and sizzling."[8]

One of Doctorow's sharpest departures from popular narrative convention is the manner in which he rewards self-serving opportunism and even outright villainy instead of punishing it, as the novelist, screenwriter, and director in the commercial arts almost always feel constrained to do. In *Ragtime*, for example, Tateh abandons his wife, his social conscience, and his religion, and yet ends up happily ever after in Hollywood. In *Loon Lake*, Joe abandons his past, his parents, his social conscience, and his child fiancée with her babe in arms and yet ends up as the millionaire Master of Loon Lake. This is perhaps one aspect of those "moral and political issues" Schiff said were buried and disregarded in the genre material from which Doctorow derives his narrative energy. Reviewing *Billy Bathgate* for *Time*, Paul Gray noted that both the adventures and the boy who tells of them "are as far as they could be from innocent visions of Tom Sawyer or Horatio Alger."[9] This lack of innocence and willingness to be exploitative marks all of Doctorow's fiction and sets it apart from mere genre stuff. His central figures come in out of the cold to "families" of one sort of another—homey and loving in some cases, criminal and outcast in other situations, aristocratic and arrogant in still other instances. Thus, Blue in *Hard Times* is a middle-aged drifter who discovers in himself a talent for the fathering of orphans, the husbanding of fire-scarred whores, and the creation of villages in the wasteland of the American high plains; in *Big as Life*, Red Bloom lives by his uncompromised jazzman's code and kids Sugarbush that "your trouble is you're not an outlaw"; Daniel Isaacson is the outlaw son of martyred parents who suicidally aspired to a higher morality than the bourgeois public life of their country could ever achieve, and he comes to see in the hippie activist Artie Sternlicht the very incarnation of late-1960s radical cool.

Ragtime, Loon Lake, and *Billy Bathgate* are all novels which in various ways investigate with contagious fascination that unique American archetype, the criminal genius. Marginal man is Doctorow's favorite subject, just as the city and the family are his laboratory. "My life is bad for my image," Doctorow told *Time*, referring to his financial success and respectability, his academic chair at

NYU, his children and his tennis, the fact that he wrote so much about crime but never in fact hung out in what he calls "lowlife saloons." "Dedicated criminals live on the extreme edge of civilization, where manners and morals unravel and the underlying impetus of our tribal, primordial origins breaks through," Doctorow has said about his fascination with criminality. "My background, which was safe and conventional, may have made me attentive to life beyond the pale."[10] The quality of events being "beyond the pale" is certainly intrinsic to *Billy Bathgate*, just as it is to so much of his fiction. But this very criminality and extremism is subject to a powerful countervailing centripetal force: the desire to belong to a family.

Billy Bathgate is not quite a successful novel, but a less ambitious writer would never have tried to bring off this bizarre tale of what Doctorow characterized as a solitary boy's "search for patrimony and justice."[11] From the crisp deadpan ironies of *Ragtime* through purple thunderclouds of *Billy Bathgate* there is no doubt that Doctorow is a writer always pushing at the far edges of his talent in an attempt to achieve work of significance and authority. *The Book of Daniel, Ragtime,* and *World's Fair* are perhaps Doctorow's greatest successes, but everything he has published demonstrates not only his talent but his restless search for a new means of expressing what Joseph Conrad considered the treasures that only fiction can bestow:

"encouragement, consolation, fear, charm—all you demand—and, perhaps, also that glimpse of truth for which you had forgotten to ask."[12]

Notes

1. Wilde's comment comes from a letter of 19 April 1882, quoted in Ron Hansen, *The Assassination of Jesse James by the Coward Robert Ford* (New York; Ballantine, 1984) 253.

2. Doctorow, *Billy Bathgate* (New York: Random House, 1989) 3. Further references will be noted parenthetically.

3. Peter S. Prescott, "Getting into Dutch," *Newsweek* 13 Feb. 1989: 76.

4. Stephen Schiff, "What's Up, Doctorow?" *Vanity Fair* Feb. 1989: 48.

5. George Orwell, *A Collection of Essays* (New York: Doubleday, 1954) 104.

6. Schiff 54.

7. Kay Bonetti, "An Interview with E. L. Doctorow, Feb. 1990" (Columbia, Mo: American Audio Prose Library).

8. Schiff 54.

9. Paul Gray, "In the Shadow of Dutch Schultz," *Time* 27 Feb. 1989: 76.

10. Interview, "Attentive to Mysteries," *Time* 27 Feb. 1989: 76.

11. Bonetti interview.

12. Conrad, preface to *The Nigger of the "Narcissus."*

BIBLIOGRAPHY

Works by Doctorow

Books

Welcome to Hard Times. New York: Simon and Schuster, 1960; *Bad Man from Bodie*. London: Deutsch, 1961.

Big as Life. New York: Simon and Schuster, 1966.

The Book of Daniel. New York: Random House, 1971; London: Macmillan, 1971.

Ragtime. New York: Random House, 1975; London: Macmillan, 1976.

Drinks Before Dinner: A Play. New York: Random House, 1979; London: Macmillan, 1980.

Loon Lake. New York: Random House, 1980; London: Macmillan, 1980.

Lives of the Poets: Six Stories and a Novella. New York: Random House, 1984; London: Michael Joseph, 1985.

World's Fair. New York: Random House, 1985; London: Michael Joseph, 1986.

Billy Bathgate. New York: Random House, 1989; London: Macmillan, 1991.

Selected Articles

"After the Nightmare." *Sports Illustrated* 28 June 1976: 72–82.

"The Bomb Lives!" *Playboy* Mar. 1974: 114–16, 208–16.

"James Wright at Kenyon." *The Gettysburg Review* 3 (Winter 1990): 11–22.

"Living in the House of Fiction." *The Nation* 23 Apr. 1978: 459–62.

Bibliography

Critical Works

Books

Friedl, Herwig, and Dieter Schulz, eds. *E. L. Doctorow. A Democracy of Perception.* Essen: Die Blau Eule, 1988. European responses to Doctorow by many hands; includes an interview in which Doctorow acknowledges his debt to Nathaniel Hawthorne and the romance narrative.

Harter, Carol C., and James R. Thompson. *E. L. Doctorow.* Boston: Twayne, 1990. Emphasizes Doctorow's various narrative intentions and his willingness to experiment; well-researched and comprehensive.

Levine, Paul. *E. L. Doctorow.* London and New York: Methuen, 1985. Excellent study centering on Doctorow's use of political themes and his social vision.

Trenner, Richard, ed. *E. L. Doctorow: Essays and Conversations.* Princeton, NJ: Ontario Review Press, 1983. Two essays by Doctorow, "For the Artist's Sake" and "False Documents," offer insight into his conception of the state's essential antagonism toward the arts and the artist and of the value of fiction as a means of stating a higher truth than other forms of discourse can provide. Three interviews with Doctorow provide biographical connections between his life and work, discussion of his political views, and extensive comments about his artistic concerns. Of the nine essays about Doctorow included, the most valuable are John Clayton's discussion of Doctorow's "radical Jewish humanism" and John Ditsky's article on the transformation of Heinrich von Kleist's *Michael Kohlhaas* into an incident in *Ragtime.*

Bibliography

Sections of Books, Uncollected Articles, Selected Reviews

Atwood, Margaret. "E. L. Doctorow: Writing by His Own Rules." *Washington Post Book World* 28 Sept. 1980: 1–2, 10. Praise from a distinguished novelist for Doctorow's "verbally dazzling" performances.

Bakker, J. "The Western: Can It Be Great?" *Dutch Quarterly Review of Anglo-American Letters,* 14 (1984): 140–63. *Welcome to Hard Times* contrasted to the standard American Western.

Cooper, Barbara. "The Artist as Historian in the Novels of E. L. Doctorow." *Emporia State Research Studies* 29 (Fall 1980): 5–44. Good discussion of Doctorow's use of the voice of a historian in his first five novels.

DeMott, Benjamin. "Doctorow's Promise." *The Atlantic Monthly* Sept. 1980: 105–07. Negative but eloquent comments on *Loon Lake.*

Emblidge, David. "Marching Backward into the Future: Progress as Illusion in Doctorow's Novels." *Southwest Review* (Autumn 1977): 397–409. Study of Doctorow's pessimism, cleverly expressed.

Epstein, Joseph. "A Conspiracy of Silence." *Harper's* Nov. 1977: 80–92. Political disagreement with Doctorow's intentions in *The Book of Daniel.* Excellent analysis of Doctorow's alterations of history for political effect and of the emotional background of American-Jewish sentiments about the Rosenberg case.

Green, Martin. "Nostalgia Politics." *American Scholar* 45 (Winter 1975/76): 841–45. A distinguished cultural commentator finds unwholesome the radical political pretensions evoked by *Ragtime.*

Hague, Angela. "*Ragtime* and the Movies." *North Dakota Quarterly* 50 (1983): 101–12. One of the best of the

Bibliography

many articles examining the "photographic" quality of Doctorow's experiments in prose and the relationship of his printed work with its film incarnations.

Harpham, Geoffrey Galt. "E. L. Doctorow and the Technology of Narrative." *PMLA* 100 (1985): 81–95. Discussion of Doctorow's various narrative strategies in postmodernist critical terminology.

Johnson, Diane. "The Righteous Artist: E. L. Doctorow." *Terrorists and Novelists,* ed. Johnson. New York: Knopf, 1982. 141–49. Discusses Doctorow's technical experimentation.

Kauffmann, Stanley. "A Central Vision." *Saturday Review* 26 July 1975: 20–22. Brilliant short discussion of *Ragtime* as a revelation of essential history beneath "official" history.

Kramer, Hilton. "Political Romance." *Commentary* Oct. 1975: 80. Dissenting opinion on *Ragtime,* objecting to the novel's radical Left bias.

Nadel, Alan. "Hero and Other in Doctorow's *Loon Lake.*" *College Literature* 14 (1987): 136–45. Doctorow's use of Nabokov, especially in the surreal conception of *Loon Lake.*

Raban, Jonathan. "Easy Virtue: On Doctorow's *Ragtime.*" *Encounter* Feb. 1976: 71–74. Finds the novel merely entertainment touched up with Leftist politics and "attractive little ideas" to give it a radical and learned air.

Schiff, Stephen. "What's Up, Doctorow?" *Vanity Fair* Feb. 1989: 48, 54. Review and retrospective, intelligently done.

Stark, John. "Alienation and Analysis in E. L. Doctorow's *The Book of Daniel.*" *Critique* 16 (1975): 101–10. Good discussion of the novel's experimental use of first- and third-person voices.

Weber, Bruce. "The Myth Maker: The Creative Mind of Novelist E. L. Doctorow." *New York Times Magazine* 21 Oct. 1985: 25–31. Engaging retrospective occasioned by publication of *World's Fair,* with interesting biographical material.

Interviews

Bonetti, Kay. "An Interview with E. L. Doctorow." 35-minute audiocassette recorded Feb. 1990. Columbia, MO: American Audio Prose Library.

Navasky, Victor. "E. L. Doctorow: I Saw a Sign." *New York Times Book Review* 28 Sept. 1980: 44–45.

Plimpton, George. "The Art of Fiction." *Paris Review* 101 (1986): 22–47.

Bibliography

Tokarczyk, Michelle M. *E. L. Doctorow: An Annotated Bibliography.* New York: Garland, 1988. Primary and secondary.

INDEX

Index

Index

172

Index

Index